S0-BSX-221

2.
Db Cm7 Bbm7 Db6 (Ebbass) Gb Db
— there, — yes, I will. — Now ain't it good to know that you've — got a friend — when
Ab Abmaj7 Db Gb7 Fm
peo-ple can be — so cold? — They'll hurt — you, yes, and de-sert — you and take your soul — if you let
Bb7 Bb9 Bbm7 (Ebbass)
D. S. al Coda
them. Oh, but don't you let — them. You just call —
mf f
Coda
Db Cm7
— there, — yes, I will. —
Bbm7 Db6 (EbBass) Ab Db (Abbass) Ab Db (Abbass)
Repeat and fade
— You've got a friend. — You've got a friend. — Ain't it good — to know you've got a

(Eb bass)
Db6
Eb
Db6 (EbBass)
Ab
Db
You just call out my name and you know wher-ev-er I am
Ab
Db6 (Ebbass)
I'll come run - nin' to see you a-gain.
Ab
Abmaj7
Db
Ab6
Ab7
To Coda
1.
Db
Cm7
Win-ter, spring, sum-mer or fall
All you have to do is call
and I'll be there.
Bbm7
Db6 (Eb bass)
Ab
Db (Ab bass)
(C bass)
Db
Ab
Bbm
Ab
Gm7
C7
NC
You've got a friend.
If the sky

YOU'VE GOT A FRIEND

Words and Music by
CAROLE KING

Copyright © 1971 by Colgems-EMI Music Inc., 6255 Sunset Blvd., Hollywood, Calif. 90028
International Copyright Secured Made in U.S.A. All Rights Reserved

4702YSMT

You've Got A Friend

Words and Music by CAROLE KING

Recorded by CAROLE KING on Ode 70 Records

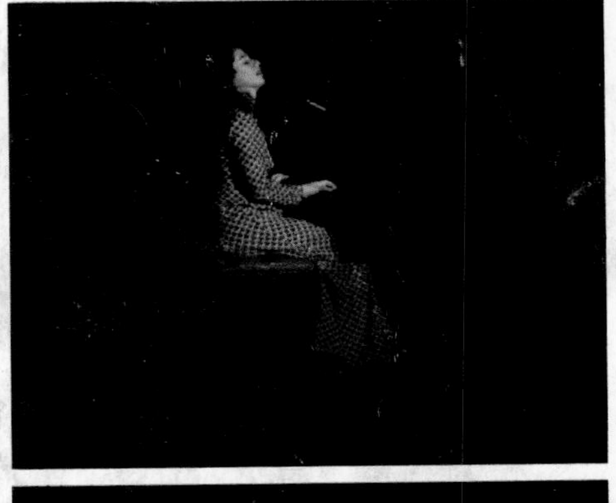

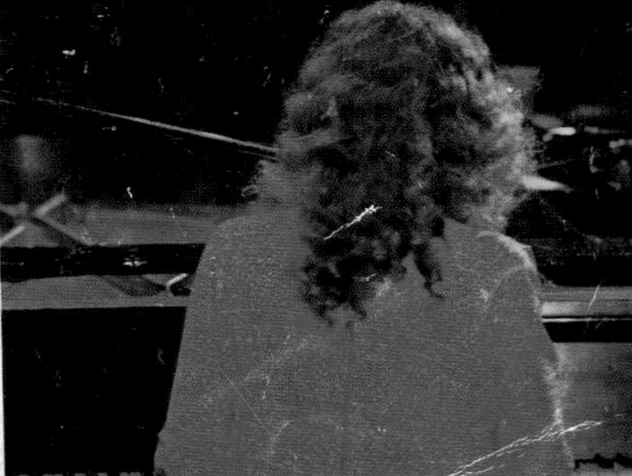

$1.95

Columbia Pictures Publications
16333 N.W. 54th Ave., Hialeah, Florida 33014

®
A Trademark of Colgems-EMI Music Inc.

COLGEMS-EMI MUSIC INC.

PIANO • VOCAL • GUITAR

SECOND EDITION

THE BEST ROCK SONGS EVER

CONTENTS

ISBN 0-7935-0071-0

7777 W. BLUEMOUND RD. P.O. BOX 13819 MILWAUKEE, WI 53213

For all works contained herein:
Unauthorized copying, arranging, adapting, recording or public performance is an infringement of copyright.
Infringers are liable under the law.

Visit Hal Leonard Online at
www.halleonard.com

ALL DAY AND ALL OF THE NIGHT

Words and Music by
RAY DAVIES

Copyright © 1964, 1965 Jayboy Music Corp.
Copyright Renewed
All Rights Administered by Sony/ATV Music Publishing, 8 Music Square West, Nashville, TN 37203
International Copyright Secured All Rights Reserved

B♭
G
F
B♭
The on - ly time I
F
A
feel al - right is by your side
Dm
C
F
D
Girl I want to be with you all of the
C
F
D
time all day and all of the night

C
To Coda
1 F D
All day and all of the night
C F D F
All day and all of the night
2 F D F
D.S. al Coda
all of the night
CODA
F D C
all of the night
All day and
F D C F D
all of the night

ALL SHOOK UP

Words and Music by OTIS BLACKWELL
and ELVIS PRESLEY

Medium Shuffle
B♭
f
B♭
A - well - a, bless my soul, what's wrong with me? I'm
itch - ing like a man on a fuz - zy tree. My friends say I'm act - in'
queer as a bug, I'm in love! I'm all shook up! Mm

Copyright © 1957 by Shalimar Music Corporation
Copyright Renewed and Assigned to Elvis Presley Music (Administered by R&H Music)
International Copyright Secured All Rights Reserved

E♭7
F7
B♭
E♭7
mm oh, oh, yeah, yeah!
B♭
My hands are shak - y and my knees are weak, I
can't seem to stand on my own two feet.
Who do you thank when you
have such luck? I'm in love!
I'm all shook up! Mm

Eb7
F7
Bb
Eb7
mm oh, oh, yeah, yeah!
Bb
Eb7
Please don't ask what's on my mind, I'm a
tongue gets tied when I try to speak, my
Bb
lit - tle mixed up but I'm feel - in' fine. When I'm
in - sides shake like a leaf on a tree. There's
Eb7
near that girl that I love best, My
on - ly one cure for this soul of mine, that's to

F7
B♭
heart beats so it scares me to death!
have the girl that I love so fine!
She touched my hand, what a
chill I got, her kiss - es are like a vol - ca - no that's hot! I'm
proud to say she's my but - ter - cup. I'm in love! I'm
E♭7
F7
all shook up! Mm mm oh, oh, yeah,

1
B♭
E♭7
B♭
2
B♭
yeah! My yeah! I'm
E♭7
F7
all shook up! Mm mm oh, oh, yeah,
B♭
E♭7
yeah! I'm all shook up! Mm mm oh,
F7
B♭
oh, yeah, yeah! I'm all shook up!

ANGIE

Words and Music by MICK JAGGER
and KEITH RICHARDS

© 1973 EMI MUSIC PUBLISHING LTD.
All Rights for the U.S. and Canada Controlled and Administered by COLGEMS-EMI MUSIC INC.
All Rights Reserved International Copyright Secured Used by Permission

C
Dm
C
G
here?
With no lov-ing in our souls and no
Dm
Am
C
F
mon-ey in our coats,
you can't stay we're sat-is-fied,
G
Am
but An-gie,
E7
G
B♭/F
F
An - gie,
you can't say we nev-er tried.

C
Dm
C
Em/B
Am
An - gie, ___ you're
E7
G
B♭/F
F
beau - ti - ful,
but ain't it time we said good-bye? _
C
Dm
C
Am
An - gie,
E7
G
B♭/F
F
I still love _ you.
Re - mem - ber all _ those nights we cried? _

C
Dm
C
G
All the dreams we held so close seemed to all
Dm
Am
C
F
go up in smoke.
Let me whis - per in your ear;
G
Am
"An - gie,
E7
G
B♭/F
F
An - gie,
where will it lead us from

C
Dm
C
Em/B
Am
here?"
E7
G
B♭/F
F
C
Dm
C
Em/B
Am
E7
G
B♭/F
F
C
Dm
C
Oh,

G
Dm
Am
An - gie, don't _ you weep, all your kiss - es still taste sweet.
C
F
G
I hate that sad - ness in _ your eyes, _ but
Am
E7
An-gie, An - gie,
G
B♭/F
F
C
Dm
C
Em/B
ain't it time _ we said good - bye? _ Oh,

Am
E7
yes.
G
B♭/F
F
C
Dm
C
With no
G
Dm
Am
lov-ing in our souls and no mon-ey in our coats,
C
F
G
you can't say we're sat-is-fied, but

Dm
Am
Angie, I still love you, baby.
Dm
Am
Ev-'ry-where I look I see your eyes.
Dm
Am
There ain't a wom-an that comes close to you.
C
F
G
Come on, ba-by, dry your eyes. But
8

Am
E7
Angie,
An - gie,
G
B♭/F
F
C
Dm
C
ain't it good to be a - live?
Am
E7
An - gie,
An - gie,
G
B♭/F
F
Em
Dm
C
they can't say we nev - er tried.

AT THE HOP

Words and Music by ARTHUR SINGER,
JOHN MADARA and DAVID WHITE

Copyright © 1957 (Renewed) by Arc Music Corporation and Six Continents Music Publishing, Inc. (BMI)
All Rights Controlled by Arc Music Corporation (BMI)
International Copyright Secured All Rights Reserved
Used by Permission

G6
rock it, you can roll it, do the stomp and e - ven stroll it at the
swing it, you can groove it, you can real - ly start to move it at the
G7
C9
hop.
When the rec - ords start a - spin - nin', you ca -
hop.
Where the jock - ey is the smooth - est and the
G6
lyp - so and you chick - en at the hop.
Do the
mu - sic is the cool - est at the hop.
All the
D7
C9
dance sen - sa - tions that are sweep - in' the na - tion at the
cats and the chicks can get their kicks at the

G6
hop.
hop.
(Spoken:) Let's go!
(Sung:) Let's go to the hop!
G7
C9
Let's go to the hop! (Oh, ba - by) Let's go to the hop! (Oh, ba - by)
G6
D7
C9
Let's go to the hop! Come on,
1
G6
let's go to the hop! Well, you can
2
G6
let's go to the hop!

BENNIE AND THE JETS

Words and Music by ELTON JOHN
and BERNIE TAUPIN

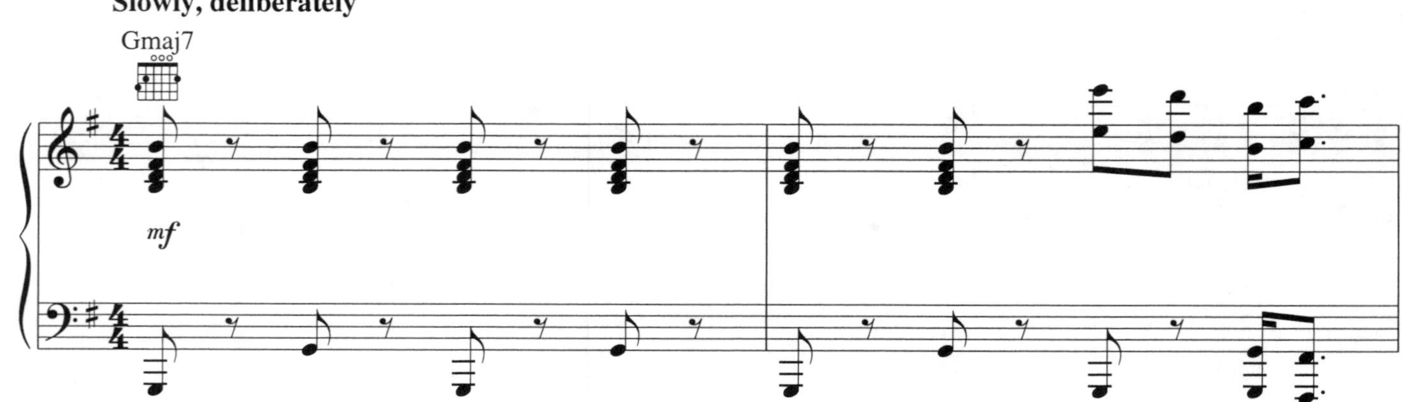
Slowly, deliberately
Gmaj7
mf

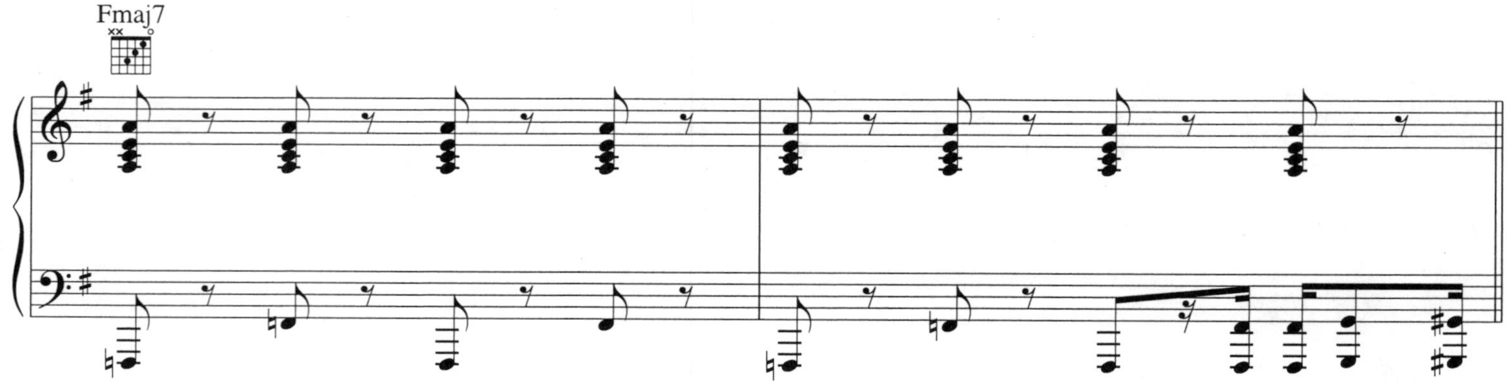
Fmaj7

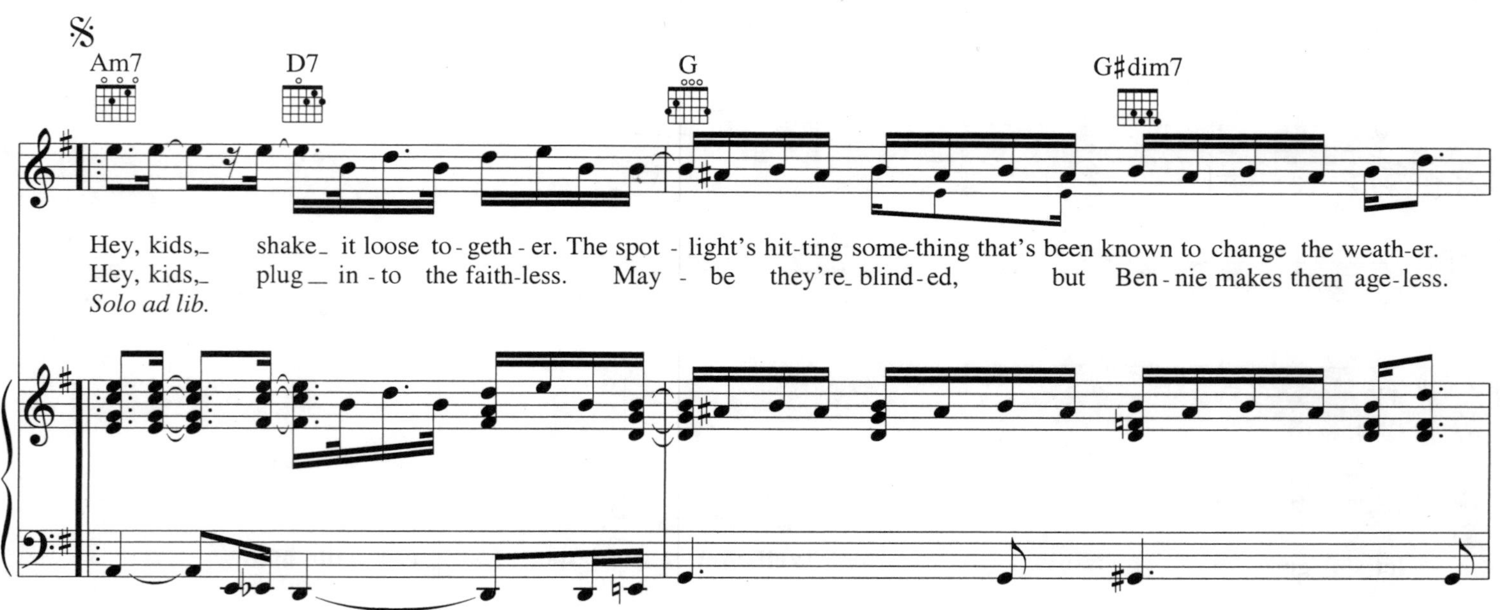
Am7
D7
G
G♯dim7
Hey, kids, shake it loose to-geth-er. The spot-light's hit-ting some-thing that's been known to change the weath-er.
Hey, kids, plug in-to the faith-less. May-be they're blind-ed, but Ben-nie makes them age-less.
Solo ad lib.

Copyright © 1973 Dick James Music Limited
All Rights for the United States and Canada Administered by Songs Of PolyGram International, Inc.
International Copyright Secured All Rights Reserved

Am7
D
Em
We'll kill the fat-ted calf to-night, so stick a-round. You're
We shall sur - vive; let us take our-selves a-long, where we
3
3
Am
Bm
C
gon-na hear e-lec - tric mu - sic sol-id walls of sound.
fight our par-ents out in the streets to find who's right and who's wrong. Say,
Solo ends
Gmaj7
Am
Can-dy and Ron - nie, have you seen them yet, ooh but they're so spaced out. B-B-B-B-B
C
Gmaj7
Ben-nie and the Jets. Oh but they're weird and they're won-der-ful. Oh, Ben -

Am
C
D
- nie, she's _ real - ly keen.
She's got e - lec - tric boots,
a mo - hair suit; ___ you know I
Em
Em/D
C
B♭/C
C
read it in a mag - a - zine, ____ oh. ____
B - B - B Ben - nie and the
Gmaj7
Jets.
Fmaj7
To Coda
1

2
D.S. al Coda
CODA
Gmaj7
Ben-nie, Ben-nie, Ben-nie, Ben-nie and the Jets.
Fmaj7
Repeat and Fade
Optional Ending
Gmaj7

BLUE SUEDE SHOES

Words and Music by
CARL LEE PERKINS

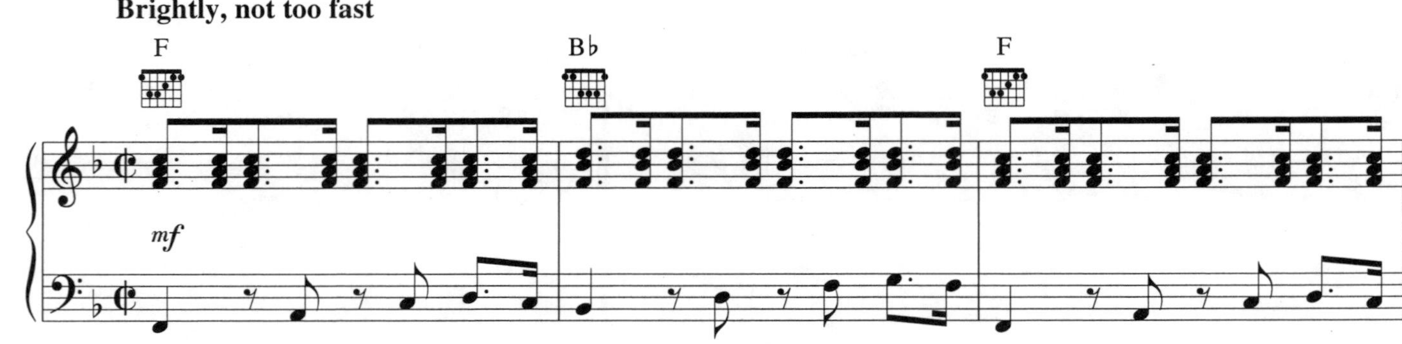
Brightly, not too fast
F
B♭
F
mf

N.C.
C
N.C.
F7
N.C.
F7
Well, it's one for the mon - ey, two for the show,

N.C.
B♭7
three to get read - y, now go, cat, go! But don't you

Copyright © 1955 by Carl Perkins Music, Inc.
Copyright Renewed
All Rights Administered by Unichappell Music Inc.
International Copyright Secured All Rights Reserved

F
step on my blue suede shoes.
You can
C
Bb
F
Bb7
do an - y - thing but lay off of my blue suede shoes.
F
C
N.C.
F7
N.C.
F7
Well, you can knock me down, step on my face,
burn my house, steal my car,
N.C.
F7
N.C.
slan - der my name all o - ver the place;
drink my ci - der from my old fruit jar;
Do an - y - thing that you

F7
N.C.
Bb7
want to do, but uh - uh, hon-ey, lay off of my shoes. Don't you
F
step on my blue suede shoes. You can
C
Bb
1
F
Bb7
do an - y - thing but lay off of my blue suede shoes.
F
C
N.C.
2
F
Bb7
F
F7#9
Well, you can shoes.

BORN TO BE WILD

Words and Music by
MARS BONFIRE

© Copyright 1968 MANITOU MUSIC CANADA, A Division of MCA CANADA LTD.
Copyright Renewed
All Rights for the USA Controlled and Administered by MUSIC CORPORATION OF AMERICA, INC.
International Copyright Secured All Rights Reserved
MCA Music Publishing

Eb
Gb
Ab
Eb
make it hap - pen, take the world in a love em - brace.
Gb
Ab
Eb
Gb
Ab
Fire all of your guns at once and ex - plode in - to space.
1
Eb
Bb
2
Eb
Like a true na-ture child we were born,
Gb
Ab
born to be wild. We have climbed so high,

G♭
E♭
D♭
nev - er want to die.
Born to be wild.
E♭
D♭
E♭
D♭
Born to be wild.
E♭
D♭
1
2
E♭
D♭
E♭
D♭
Repeat and Fade
Born to be wild.

BO DIDDLEY

Words and Music by
ELLAS McDANIEL

Brightly *(a la Calypso)*

f

G

mp

Bo Did-dley'll buy ba-by a dia - mond ring,

G6 G G6

If that dia - mond ring don't shine,

G G6

He's gon-na take it to a pri - vate eye.

Copyright © 1955 (Renewed) by Arc Music Corporation (BMI)
International Copyright Secured All Rights Reserved
Used by Permission

G G6 G

If that pri-vate eye can't see, He bet-ter not take that

Dm7 G

ring from me. Bo Did-dl-ey caught a nan-ny goat,

To make his pret-ty ba-by a Sun-day coat.

R.H.

Bo Did-dl-ey caught a bear - cat,

R.H.

R.H.
To make his pret - ty ba - by a Sun - day hat.
Dm7
G
Dm7
G
Dm7
ff
G
Guitar Tacet
G6
mf
G
G6
Won't you come to my house and rack that bone,
mp

G G6 G

Take my ba-by all the way from home. Look at that bo-do, Oh,

G6 G

where's he been, Up to your house and gone a-gain.

G6 G

Bo Did-dl-ey, Bo Did-dl-ey, have you heard,

R.H.

My pret-ty ba-by said she was a bird.

R.H.

Repeat and Fade

THE BOYS ARE BACK IN TOWN

Words and Music by
PHILIP PARRIS LYNOTT

Copyright © 1976 by Pippin-The-Friendly-Ranger Music Co. Ltd.
All Rights Administered by PolyGram International Publishing, Inc.
International Copyright Secured All Rights Reserved

Bm C E♭

were a - round, How you was, ___ where you could be found. ___

Bm Em Am

I told them you were liv - ing down - town, Driv - ing all the old men

Am/D G(no3rd)

Chorus

cra - zy. The boys are back in town, the boys are back in town.

A(no3rd) C(no 3rd) G(no3rd)

I say, the boys are back in town, ___ the

A(no3rd)
C(no 3rd)
G(no3rd)
boys are back in town. The boys are back in town, the
A(no3rd)
C(no 3rd)
boys are back in town, the boys are back in town, the boys are back in town.
G
G/B
Am/D
(Fade after 3rd Chorus)
G
G/B
Am/D

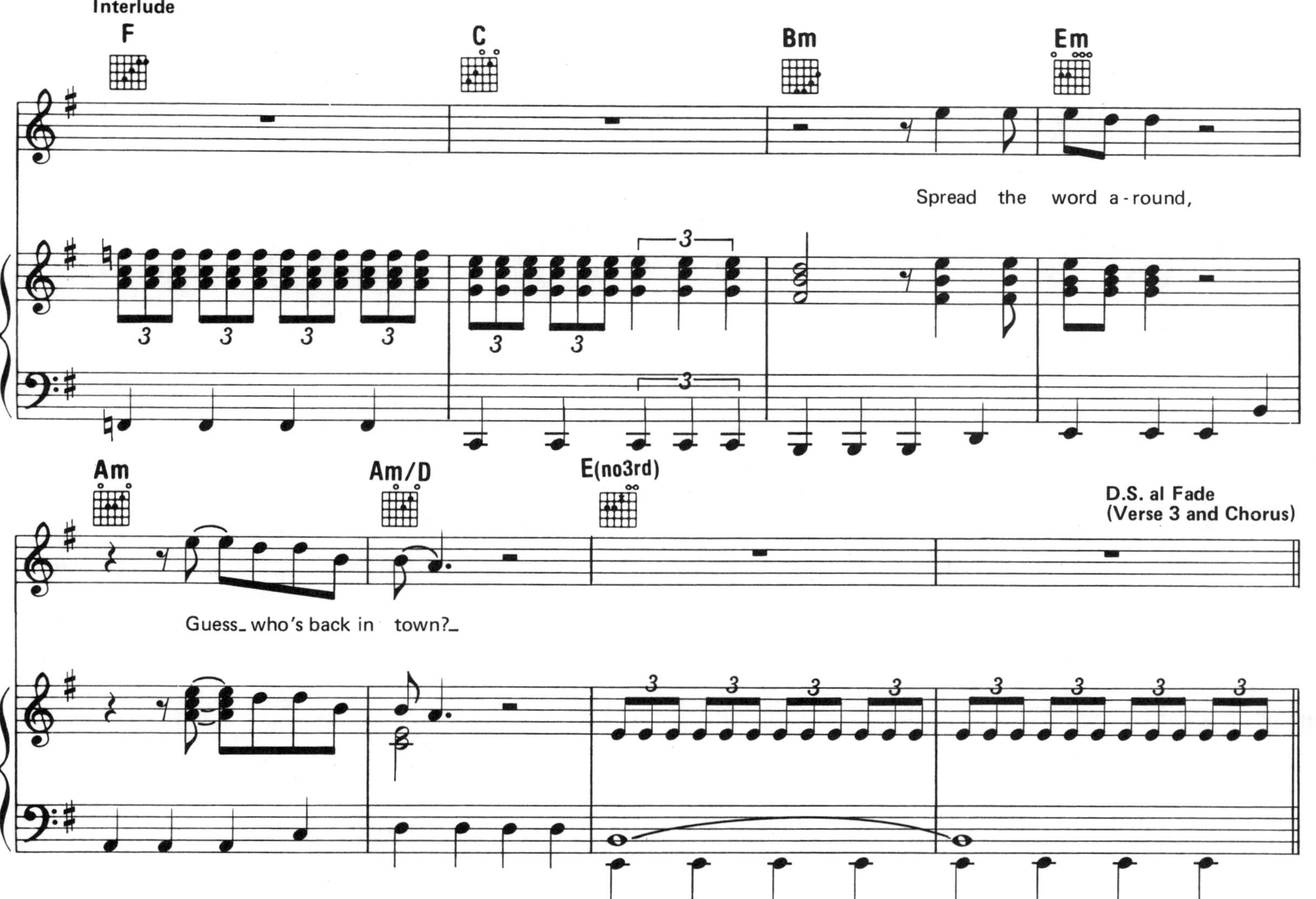

Additional Verses:

2. You know that chick that used to dance a lot
Every night she'd be on the floor shaking what she'd got
Man, when I tell you she was cool, she was hot
I mean she was steaming.

And that time over at Johnny's place
Well, this chick got up and she slapped Johnny's face
Man, we just fell about the place
If that chick don't wanna know, forget her.

(Chorus & Interlude)

3. Friday night they'll be dressed to kill
Down at Dino's Bar and Grill
The drink will flow and blood will spill
And if the boys want to fight, you better let 'em

That jukebox in the corner blasting out my favorite song
The nights are getting warmer, it won't be long
It won't be long till summer comes
Now that the boys are here again.

(Chorus and Fade)

BROWN EYED GIRL

Words and Music by
VAN MORRISON

Copyright © 1967 Songs Of PolyGram International, Inc.
Copyright Renewed
International Copyright Secured All Rights Reserved

E♭
B♭7
E♭
A♭
skip-ping and a jump-ing. In the mis - ty morn - ing fog with
E♭
B♭7
A♭
B♭7
our hearts a-thump - in', and you, my brown eyed
E♭
Cm
A♭
B♭7
girl. You, my brown eyed girl.
E♭
B♭7
Do you re-mem - ber when we used to sing:

Additional Lyrics

2. Whatever happened to Tuesday and so slow
Going down the old mine with a transistor radio
Standing in the sunlight laughing
Hiding behind a rainbow's wall
Slipping and a-sliding
All along the water fall
With you, my brown eyed girl
You, my brown eyed girl.
Do you remember when we used to sing:
Chorus

3. So hard to find my way, now that I'm all on my own
I saw you just the other day, my, how you have grown
Cast my memory back there, Lord
Sometime I'm overcome thinking 'bout
Making love in the green grass
Behind the stadium
With you, my brown eyed girl
With you, my brown eyed girl.
Do you remember when we used to sing:
Chorus

CALIFORNIA DREAMIN'

Words and Music by JOHN PHILLIPS
and MICHELLE PHILLIPS

© Copyright 1965, 1970 by MCA MUSIC PUBLISHING, A Division of UNIVERSAL STUDIOS, INC.
Copyright Renewed
International Copyright Secured All Rights Reserved
MCA Music Publishing

E7 Am G F G Bm7
To Coda
Cal - i - for - nia dream-in' On such a win-ter's day.
E7 Am G F G Bm7
Stopped in - to a church, I passed a - long the way.
E7 F C E7 Am F E Dm6
Oh, I got down on my knees, And I pre - tend to pray.
E7 Am G F G Bm7
You know the preach-er likes the cold, He knows I'm gon - na stay.
3
3

E7
Am
G
F
G
Cal - i - for - nia dream - in'
On such a win - ter's
Bm7
E7
D.S. al Coda
day.
All the leaves are
CODA
F
G
On such a win - ter's
Am
G
F
G
Am
G
F
G
day. (Cal - i - for - nia dream - in') On such a win - ter's day. (Cal - i - for - nia dream - in') On such a win - ter's
Fmaj7
Am
day.

CHANTILLY LACE

Words and Music by
J.P. RICHARDSON

Moderate Boogie Woogie

C7

mf

F

C7

(Ha - ha - ha - ha - ha)

Spoken: Oh,

F

F7

you sweet thing!

Do I what?

Bb

F

Will I what?

Copyright © 1958 Glad Music Co.
Copyright Renewed and Assigned to Fort Knox Music Inc., Trio Music Co., Inc. and Glad Music Co.
International Copyright Secured All Rights Reserved
Used by Permission

C7
Oh, Baby, you know what I like!
F
C7
Chan - til - ly lace___ and a pret - ty face___
f
mp
F
and a pon - y tail___ hang - in' down,___ Wig - gle in her
C7
F
walk and a gig - gle in her talk, Makes the world go 'round___

F7
Bb
Ain't nothin' in this world like a big eyed girl to make me
F
C7
act so fun - ny, make me spend my mon - ey, make me feel real loose like a
1 F
Guitar Tacet
long - necked goose, like a girl. Spoken: Oh, Baby, that's - a what I like.
mf
2 F
girl. Spoken: Oh, Baby, that's - a what I like.
f

CROCODILE ROCK

Words and Music by ELTON JOHN
and BERNIE TAUPIN

Light-hearted Rock
G/D
C/E
F♯
G
f
8vb
Em
C
D
I re - mem -
G
Bm
(1., 3.) - ber when rock was young. Me and Su - sie had so much fun
went by and rock just died. Su - sie went and left us for some

Copyright © 1972 Dick James Music Limited
All Rights for the United States and Canada Administered by Songs Of PolyGram International, Inc.
International Copyright Secured All Rights Reserved

C
hold - in' hands and skim-min' stones. Had an old
for - eign guy. Long nights cry - in' by the rec - ord ma - chine, dream -
D
G
gold Chev - y and a place of my own. But the big - gest kick I ev - er got
- in' of my Chev - y and my old blue jeans. But they'll nev - er kill the thrills we've got
Bm
was do-in' a thing called the croc - o - dile rock. While the oth -
burn - ing up to the croc - o - dile rock. Learn-ing fast
C
D
- er kids were rock - in' round the clock, we were hop - pin' and bop - pin' to the
as the weeks went past, we real - ly thought the croc - o - dile

Em
croc - o - dile rock. Well,
rock _ would last. Well,
croc-o-dile rock - in' is some - thing shock - in' when your
A7
D7
feet just can't keep still. _ I nev - er knew me a
G
bet - ter time _ and I guess _ I nev - er _ will. _ Oh, _
E7
A7
_ Lord - y, ma - ma, those Fri - day nights _ when Su - sie wore _ her

D7
dress - es tight and the croc-o-dile rock - in' was out of
F/C
C
F/C
C
F/C
C
G
sight.
La,
la la la la
Em
la,
la la la la
C
la,
la la la la
D
la.

1,2
3
But the years
I re - mem -
G
Em
La,
la la la la la,
la la la la la,
C
la la la la
Repeat and Fade
D
la.
Optional Ending
D
F
F#
G
la.

DUKE OF EARL

Words and Music by EARL EDWARDS,
EUGENE DIXON and BERNICE WILLIAMS

Copyright © 1961, 1968 (Renewed) by Conrad Music, a division of Arc Music Corp. (BMI)
International Copyright Secured All Rights Reserved
Used by Permission

Ab
4 fr.
Bb7
6fr.
Eb
6fr.
no one can hurt you, Yes I'm gon-na
par-a-dise we will share, I'm gon-na
Cm
3fr.
Ab
4 fr.
love you let me hold you, 'Cause I'm the Duke of
love you let me hold you, 'Cause I'm the Duke of
1 Bb
6fr.
2 Bb
6fr.
Earl.
Earl.
Eb
6fr.
Cm
3fr.
Ab
4 fr.
Bb
6fr.
Eb
6fr.

DUST IN THE WIND

Words and Music by
KERRY LIVGREN

© 1977, 1978 EMI BLACKWOOD MUSIC INC. and DON KIRSHNER MUSIC
All Rights Controlled and Administered by EMI BLACKWOOD MUSIC INC.
All Rights Reserved International Copyright Secured Used by Permission

C
G/B
Am
All my dreams
All we do
slips a - way.
G
Dm7
Am
To Coda
pass be - fore my eyes, a cu - ri - os - i - ty.
crum - bles to the ground though we re - fuse to see.
All your mon - ey won't an - oth - er min - ute buy.
D/F♯
G
Am
Am/G
Dust in the wind.
Dust in the wind.
1
D/F♯
G
Am
G/B
All they are is dust in the wind.

2
D/F♯
G
Am
All we are is dust in the wind.
G/A
F/A
Oh
Am
G/A
F/A

C
Am
D.S. al Coda
G/B
CODA
D/F♯
G
Dust in the
Am
Am/G
D/F♯
G
wind.
(All we are is dust in the

Am
Am/G
D/F#
G
wind.)
All we are is dust in the wind.
(Dust in the
Am
Am/G
D/F#
G
wind.)
Ev - 'ry - thing is dust in the wind.
(Ev - 'ry - thing is dust in the
Am
wind.)
Am
Repeat and Fade

EVERY BREATH YOU TAKE

Written and Composed by
STING

© 1983 G.M. SUMNER
Published by MAGNETIC PUBLISHING LTD. and Administered by EMI BLACKWOOD MUSIC INC. in the USA and Canada
All Rights Reserved International Copyright Secured Used by Permission

Dsus
Em
D7sus
G
I'll be watch-ing you.
Ev - 'ry sin - gle day
Em
ev - 'ry word you say,
ev - 'ry game you play
C
D
Dsus
G
ev - 'ry night you stay,
I'll be watch-ing you.
C
C/B♭
Am7
G
Oh, can't you see
you be - long to me.

A7
How my poor heart aches with ev-'ry step you
D
D7sus
G
take. Ev-'ry move you make Ev-'ry vow you
Em
C
break, ev-'ry smile you fake ev-'ry claim you stake,
D
Dsus
Em
To Coda
I'll be watch-ing you.

Eb
F
Since you've gone I been lost with - out a trace,
I dream at night I can on - ly see your face.
I look a - round but it's you I can't re - place,
I feel so cold and I long for your em - brace.
I keep cry - ing bab - y bab - y please.
G
Em

C
D
Em
G
D.S. al Coda
CODA
Em
C
Oh can't you
Ev - 'ry move you make Ev - 'ry step you take,
D
Dsus
Em
I'll be watch - ing you.
D7sus
G
I'll be watch - ing you.

FREE BIRD

Words and Music by ALLEN COLLINS
and RONNIE VAN ZANT

© Copyright 1973, 1975 by MCA - DUCHESS MUSIC CORPORATION and WINDSWEPT PACIFIC ENTERTAINMENT CO. d/b/a LONGITUDE MUSIC CO.
All Rights Controlled and Administered by MCA - DUCHESS MUSIC CORPORATION
International Copyright Secured All Rights Reserved
MCA Music Publishing

G
D/F#
Em
For I must be trav - 'ling on now
But please don't take it so bad - ly
F
C
D
'cause there's too man - y plac - es I've got to see.
'cause the Lord knows I'm to blame.
G
D/F#
Em
But if I stayed here with you, girl,
F
C
D
things just could - n't be the same.

G
D/F#
Em
'Cause I'm as free as a bird now,
F
C
Dsus
D
Dsus
D
And this bird you'll nev - er change,
F
C
D
And this bird you can - not change,
F
C
D
And this bird you can - not change.

F
C
D
To Coda
Lord knows I can't change.
G
D/F♯
Em
(Instrumental)
F
C
1 D
2 D
D.C. al Coda
CODA
F
C
D
Lord, help me, I can't change.

GIMME SOME LOVIN'

Words and Music by SPENCER DAVIS,
MUFF WINWOOD and STEVE WINWOOD

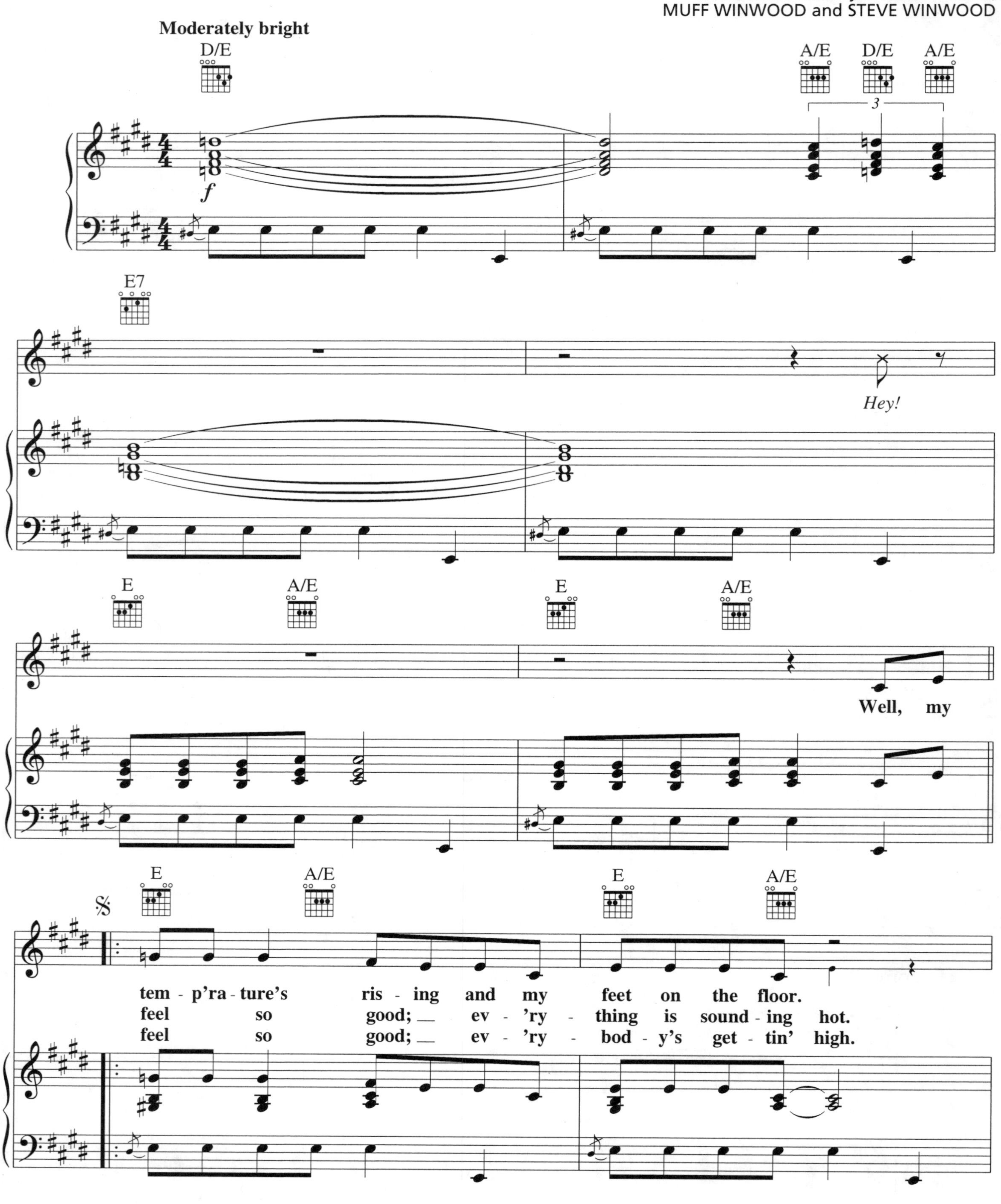

Moderately bright

D/E

E7

Hey!

E A/E E A/E

Well, my

E A/E E A/E

tem - p'ra - ture's ris - ing and my feet on the floor.
feel so good; __ ev - 'ry - thing is sound - ing hot.
feel so good; __ ev - 'ry - bod - y's get - tin' high.

Copyright © 1967 Island Music Ltd. and F.S. Music Ltd.
Copyright Renewed
All Rights for Island Music Ltd. in the U.S. and Canada Administered by Songs Of PolyGram International, Inc.
All Rights for F.S. Music Ltd. in the U.S. and Canada Administered by Warner-Tamerlane Publishing Corp.
International Copyright Secured All Rights Reserved

E
A/E
E
A/E
Twenty people knockin' 'cause they're wanting some more.
Better take it easy, 'cause the place is on fire.
Better take it easy, 'cause the place is on fire.
E
A/E
E
A/E
Let me in, baby, I don't know what you've got. But you'd
Been a hard day and I don't know what to do.
Been a hard day, nothin' went too good. Now I'm
E
A/E
E
A/E
better take it easy. This place is hot.
Wait a minute, baby. It could happen to you.
gonna relax, honey. Ev'rybody should.
E
G
So glad we made it,

A
C
E
A/E
so glad _ we made _ it. You got - ta gim-me some
lov - in',
gim - me some lov - in',
To Coda
E
A/E
gim - me some lov - in' ev - er - y day.
D/E
A/E D/E A/E
3

E7
E
A/E
Hey!
1
E
A/E
Well, I
2
E
A/E
D.S. al Coda
Well, I
CODA
E
A/E
gim - me some lov - in,'
E
A/E
Repeat and Fade
gim - me some lov - in,'

GLORIA

Words and Music by
VAN MORRISON

Copyright © 1965 by January Music Corp. and Hyde Park Music Company Ltd.
Copyright Renewed
Published in the U.S.A. and Canada by Unichappell Music Inc. and Bernice Music, Inc.
All Rights Administered by Unichappell Music Inc.
International Copyright Secured All Rights Reserved

C Bb F C Bb F C Bb F C Bb F
night. She makes me feel so good Lord, makes me feel al -
house. She knocks up - on my door, makes me feel al -
C Bb F C Bb F C Bb F C Bb F
right.
right.
Her name is G l
C Bb F C Bb F C Bb F C Bb F
o r i a
C Bb F C Bb F C Bb F
G l o r i a G l o r i
Glo - ri - a

C Bb F C Bb F C Bb F
a
G l o r i a
a
Glo - ri - a
Glo - ri -
C Bb F C Bb F C Bb F C Bb F
Al - right one time.
a Glo - ri - a Glo - ri -
C Bb F C Bb F C Bb F C Bb F
a.
1 C Bb F C Bb F
Yeah, she comes a - round
2 C Bb F C

GOOD LOVIN'

Words and Music by RUDY CLARK
and ARTHUR RESNICK

Copyright © 1965 by Alley Music Corp. and Trio Music Co., Inc.
Copyright Renewed
International Copyright Secured All Rights Reserved
Used by Permission

C F G F C F G F
now. I said, "Now doc - tor, (doc - tor) Mis - ter M.
right? I said, "Now ba - by) (ba - by) woah it's for
C F G F C F G F
D. (doc - tor) woah can you tell me (doc - tor) what's ail - ing
sure. (ba - by) I got the fe - ver (ba - by) you got the
C F G F C F/C C F/C C
me?" (doc - tor) He said, "Yeah, yeah, yeah, yeah, yeah
cure. (ba - by) She said, "Yeah, yeah, yeah, yeah, yeah
f
C F/C C F/C C D7
(yeah, yeah, yeah, yeah, yeah) all you need all you
(yeah, yeah, yeah, yeah, yeah) all you need all you

G7
F
C
F
G
F
real - ly___ need___
real - ly need___
good lov - in.'" 'Cause you got___ to have love. Good
f
C
F
G
F
C
F
G
F
To Coda
lov - in', ev' - ry bod - y got___ to have love. Good lov - in' lit - tle bit of love.___ Now ba - by good
hey now you
C
F
G
F
G
F
C
F
G
1
love.
So, come on ba -
2
D.S. (3rd ending)
3
D.S. al Coda (1st verse)
Oh,___ I was feel -
CODA
C
F
G
F
Repeat and Fade
lov - in'. Say a - gain___ now Good
f

GREAT BALLS OF FIRE

Words and Music by OTIS BLACKWELL
and JACK HAMMER

Copyright © 1957 by Chappell & Co. and Unichappell Music Inc.
Copyright Renewed
International Copyright Secured All Rights Reserved

G7
F7
me, hon-ey.
I changed my mind,
love's just fine.
C
no chord
F7
Good - ness gra - cious, great balls of fire!
Instrumental ends
Kiss me, ba - by.
Woo,
C
F7
it feels good.
Hold me, ba - by.
G7
Girl, just let me love you like a lov - er should.
I want to love you like a lov - er should.
You're fine,

so kind, I'm gon-na tell the world that you're mine, mine, mine, mine.
C
F7
I chew my nails and I twid-dle my thumb. I'm real ner-vous but it
G7
F7
sure is fun. Come on, ba-by, you're driv-ing me cra-zy.
1
C
no chord
Good-ness gra-cious, great balls of fire!
2
C
no chord
C
Good-ness gra-cious, great balls of fire!

HEARTBREAK HOTEL

Words and Music by MAE BOREN AXTON,
TOMMY DURDEN and ELVIS PRESLEY

Copyright © 1956 Sony/ATV Songs LLC
Copyright Renewed
All Rights Administered by Sony/ATV Music Publishing, 8 Music Square West, Nashville, TN 37203
International Copyright Secured All Rights Reserved

E7
N.C.
E7
(D.S.) though it's al - ways crowd - ed, you still can find ___ some room for
bell-hop's tears ___ keep flow - ing and the desk clerk's dressed _ in black. Well, they
N.C.
E7
bro - ken - heart - ed lov - ers ___ to cry there in the gloom. _ You'll be so
been so long ___ on Lone - ly Street they'll nev - er, nev - er look back. It'll make you so,
A7
B7
To Coda
it'll make you so lone - ly, ba - by. It'll make you so lone - ly. Oh, they're so lone - ly ___ they could
it'll make you so lone - ly, ba - by. Well, they're so lone - ly. Oh, they're so lone - ly ___ they could
1
2
E
E
E7
die. Now the die. Well, now if your ___ ba - by leaves you and you've
Instrumental solo

N.C.
E7
got a tale to tell, well, just take a walk down Lone - ly Street to
E7
A7
Heart - break Ho - tel where you will be, you will be so lone - ly, ba - by.
B7
1
E
Well, you'll be lone - ly. You'll be so lone - ly you could die.
2
E
D.S. al Coda
Solo ends Al -
CODA
E
F7
E7
die.

HANG ON SLOOPY

Words and Music by WES FARRELL
and BERT RUSSELL

Copyright © 1964 by Morris Music, Inc. and Sloopy II, Inc. in the U.S.
Copyright Renewed
All Rights outside the U.S. Administered by Morris Music, Inc.
International Copyright Secured All Rights Reserved

C7
Bb
F7
on,
Say Yeah, Yeah, Yeah,
Yeah, Yeah, Yeah,
Good,
Good, Good, Good, Good,
R.H.
R.H.
Good, Good, Good,
Good, Good, Good, Good.
Good, Good, Good, Good.
Good.
Oh, I wan-na say Ah
R.H.
cresc.
F7
Now I want you to
mp
F
tell me some-thing ba-by. Well don't it make you feel cra-zy. I wan-na say
F7
D.C. and Fade
Ah
cresc.

HEY JUDE

Words and Music by JOHN LENNON
and PAUL McCARTNEY

Copyright © 1968 SONY/ATV Songs LLC
Copyright Renewed
All Rights Administered by Sony/ATV Music Publishing, 8 Music Square West, Nashville, TN 37203
International Copyright Secured All Rights Reserved

C7
F
to make it better. Hey
F
C
C7
C7sus
C7
Jude, don't be a - fraid. You were made to go out and
Jude, don't let me down. You have found her, now go and
get her. The min - ute you let her un - der your
get her. Re - mem - ber to let her in - to your
F
B♭
F
C7
F
skin, then you be - gin to make it bet - ter.
heart; then you can start to make it bet - ter.

F7
B♭
B♭/A
And an - y - time you feel the pain, hey Jude, re - frain;
So let it out and let it in. Hey Jude, be - gin;
Gm7
Gm7/F
C7/E
C7
F
don't car - ry the world up - on your shoul - ders.
you're wait - ing for some - one to per - form with.
F7
B♭
B♭/A
For well you know that it's a fool who plays it cool
And don't you know that it's just you? Hey Jude, you'll do.
Gm7
Gm7/F
C7/E
C7
by mak - ing his world a lit - tle cold -
The move - ment you need is on your shoul -

F
F7
C7
er.
der.
Da da da da da da da da da.
1
2
D.S. al Coda
Hey
Hey Jude,
CODA
C7
to make it bet -
F
F
ter, bet - ter, bet - ter, bet - ter, bet - ter, bet - ter, oh.
Da da da
E♭
3 fr
B♭
F
Repeat and Fade
Optional Ending
da da da da,
da da da da,
hey Jude.

HOUND DOG

Words and Music by JERRY LEIBER
and MIKE STOLLER

Medium Rock

Copyright © 1956 by Elvis Presley Music, Inc. and Lion Publishing Co., Inc.
Copyright Renewed, Assigned to Gladys Music (Administered by Williamson Music) and MCA Music Publishing, A Division of Universal Studios, Inc.
International Copyright Secured All Rights Reserved

B♭7
cry - in' all the time.
Well, you ain't
F7
nev - er caught a rab - bit and you ain't no friend of
E♭7
B♭
(tacet)
mine.
When they said you was high - classed,
B♭7
well, that was just a lie.
When they said you was

Eb7
high - classed,
Well, that was just a
Bb
lie.
Well, you ain't
F7
ne - ver caught a rab - bit and you
Eb7
ain't no friend of
1 Bb
mine
(tacet)
You ain't noth - in' but a
2 Bb
Eb7
Bb
mine.
ped.

I SHOT THE SHERIFF

Words and Music by
BOB MARLEY

Copyright © 1974 Fifty-Six Hope Road Music Ltd. and Odnil Music Ltd.
All Rights for the United States and Canada Administered by PolyGram International Publishing, Inc.
International Copyright Secured All Rights Reserved

Gm
3 fr
Eb maj7
Dm7
home - town, they're try - ing to track me down. They
hat - ed me; for what, I don't know. And
say they want to bring me in guilt - y for the kill - ing of a dep - u -
ev - 'ry time that I plant a seed, he said, "Kill it be - fore it
ty, for the life of a dep - u - ty. But I say:
grows." He said, "Kill it be - fore it grows." But I say:
N.C.

Gm
Cm
Gm
I shot the sher - iff, but I swear it was in self - de-fense.
I shot the sher - iff, but I did not shoot the dep - u - ty.
Cm
I shot the sher - iff, but I swear it was in
I shot the sher - iff, but I did - n't shoot the
Gm
E♭maj7
Dm7
self - de-fense. (1., D.S.) Free-dom came my way one
dep - u - ty. Re - flex - es get the bet -
Gm
E♭maj7
Dm7
day, and I start - ed out of
ter of me, and what is to be must

Gm
E♭maj7
Dm7
Gm
town, yeah.
be.
All of a sud-den, I see Sher-iff John Brown
Ev-'ry day the buck-et goes to the well,
E♭maj7
Dm7
Gm
E♭maj7
Dm7
aim-ing to shoot me down,
so I shot, I shot him
but one day the bot-tom will drop out.
Yes, one day the bot-tom will
Gm
N.C.
down.
drop out.
But I say:
1

2
Gm
3 fr
Cm
3 fr
I shot the sher - iff,
but I did - n't shoot the
Gm
3 fr
dep - u - ty.
I shot the sher - iff,
Cm
3 fr
Gm
3 fr
D.S. and Fade
but I did not shoot no dep - u - ty.
Optional Ending
N.C.

I LOVE ROCK 'N' ROLL

Words and Music by ALAN MERRILL
and JAKE HOOKER

Moderately
E5
A5
5 fr
R.H.
f
L.H.
B5
E5
A5
5 fr
B5
E5
N.C.
E5
I saw him danc - ing there by the rec - ord ma -
smiled, so I got up and asked for his
8va

Copyright © 1975, 1982 Rak Publishing Ltd. for the World
All Rights for the U.S.A. and Canada Controlled by Finchley Music Corp.
Administered by Music & Media International
International Copyright Secured All Rights Reserved

E5
N.C.
chine.
I knew he must have been
name.
"That don't mat - ter," he
8va
loco
8va
B5
N.C.
a - bout sev - en - teen.
The
said, "'cause it's all the same."
I
loco
A5
5 fr
B5
E5
beat was go - ing strong,
play - ing my fa - v'rite
said, "Can I take you home
where we can be a -
said, "Can I take you home
where we can be a -
8va
A5
5 fr
song,
and I could tell it would - n't be long
lone?"
And next, we were mov - ing
lone?"
Next we were mov - ing

N.C.
till he was with me, yeah, me. And I could
on, and he was with me, yeah, me. And
on, and he was with me, yeah, me. And we'll be
B5
tell it would-n't be long till he was with me, yeah,
next we were mov-ing on, and he was with me, yeah,
mov - ing on and sing - in' that same old song, yeah, with
E5
me, sing - in',
me, sing - in',
me, sing - in',
"I love rock 'n' roll, so
A5
5 fr
B5
To Coda
E5
put an - oth - er dime in the juke - box, ba - by. I love

A5
5 fr
B5
rock 'n' roll, __ so come and take your time and dance with
E5
me."
1
N.C.
He
2
N.C.
D.S. al Coda
I
CODA
E5
I love
A5
5 fr
B5
E5
rock 'n' roll, __ so come and take your time and dance with me."

IMAGINE

© 1971 LENONO MUSIC
All Rights Controlled and Administered by EMI BLACKWOOD MUSIC INC.
All Rights Reserved International Copyright Secured Used by Permission

F
C
Cmaj7
a-bove us on - ly sky.
F
Am/E
Im-ag-ine all the peo -
Dm7
F/C
G
C/G
ple
liv - ing for to - day.
G7
C
Cmaj7
Ah.
Im - ag - ine there's no coun -

F
C
Cmaj7
tries.
ions.
It is-n't hard to do.
I won-der if you can.
F
C
Cmaj7
Noth-ing to kill or die
No need for greed or hun -
F
C
Cmaj7
3
for
ger,
and no re - li - gion, too.
a broth-er - hood of man.
3

F
Am/E
Im - ag - ine all the peo -
Im - ag - ine all the peo -
Dm7
F/C
G
C/G
ple
ple
liv - ing life in peace.
shar - ing all the world.
G7
F
G
You
you may say
I'm a
C
E7
F
G
dream - er.
But I'm not the on - ly one.

C
E7
F
G
I hope some day you'll
C
E7
F
G
join us
and the world will
C
Cmaj7
be as one.
Im - ag - ine no pos - ses -
F
G
C
and the world will live as one.
rit.

JESUS IS JUST ALRIGHT

Words and Music by
ARTHUR REYNOLDS

Bright Rock

no chord

Do do do do___ do do___ do do.___ Do do do do___ do do___

Copyright © 1969 by Artists Music, Inc. and Music Sales Corporation
Copyright Renewed
All Rights for Artists Music, Inc. Administered by BMG Songs, Inc.
International Copyright Secured All Rights Reserved

no chord
Am7
Jesus is just alright with me.
Jesus is just alright,
Em7
woh yeah.
Am7
Jesus is just alright with me.
Jesus is just alright.
E7#9
F9/E
E7#9

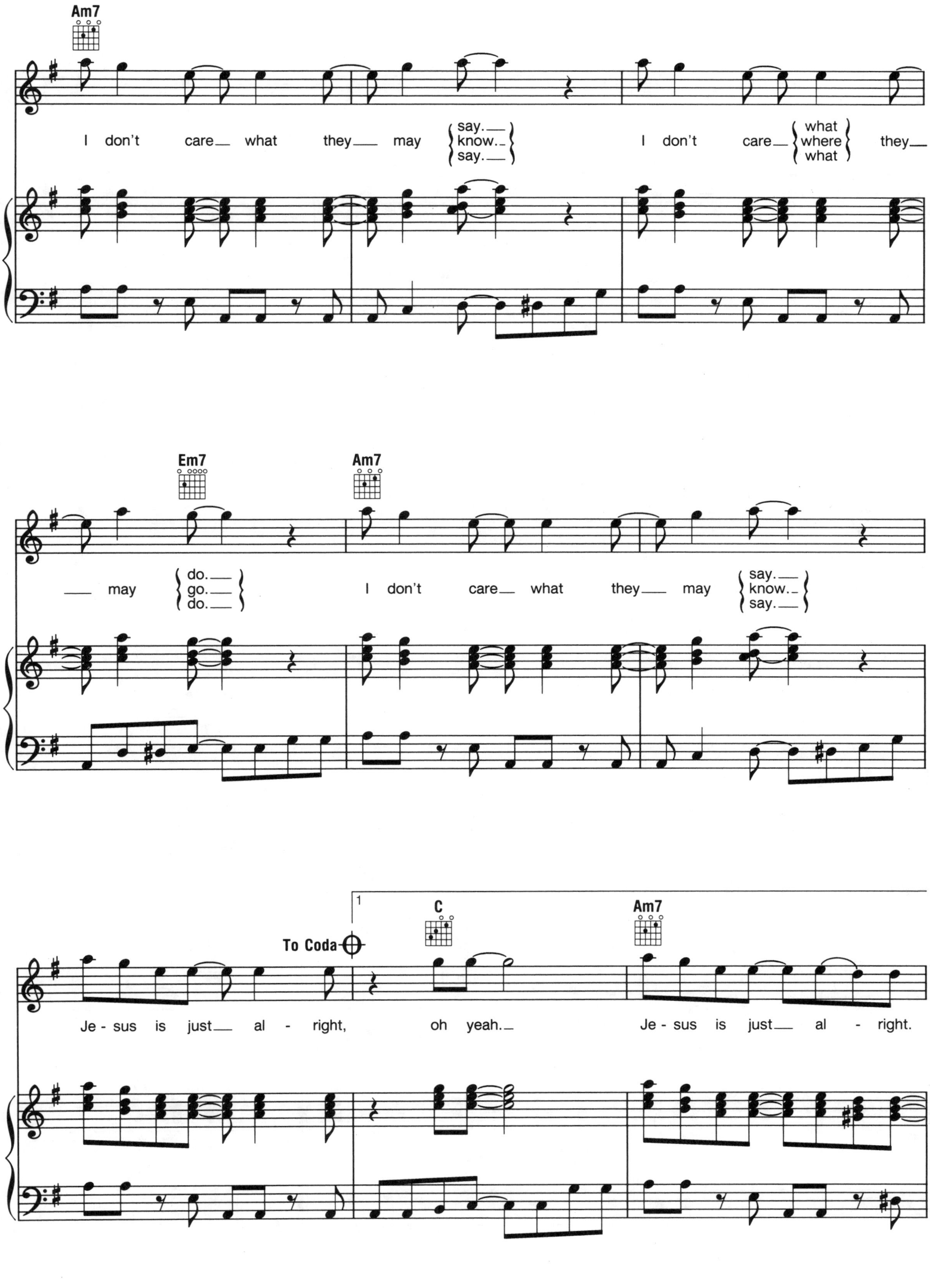

Am7

I don't care what they may {say. / know. / say.} I don't care {what / where / what} they may {do. / go. / do.}

Em7

Am7

I don't care what they may {say. / know. / say.}

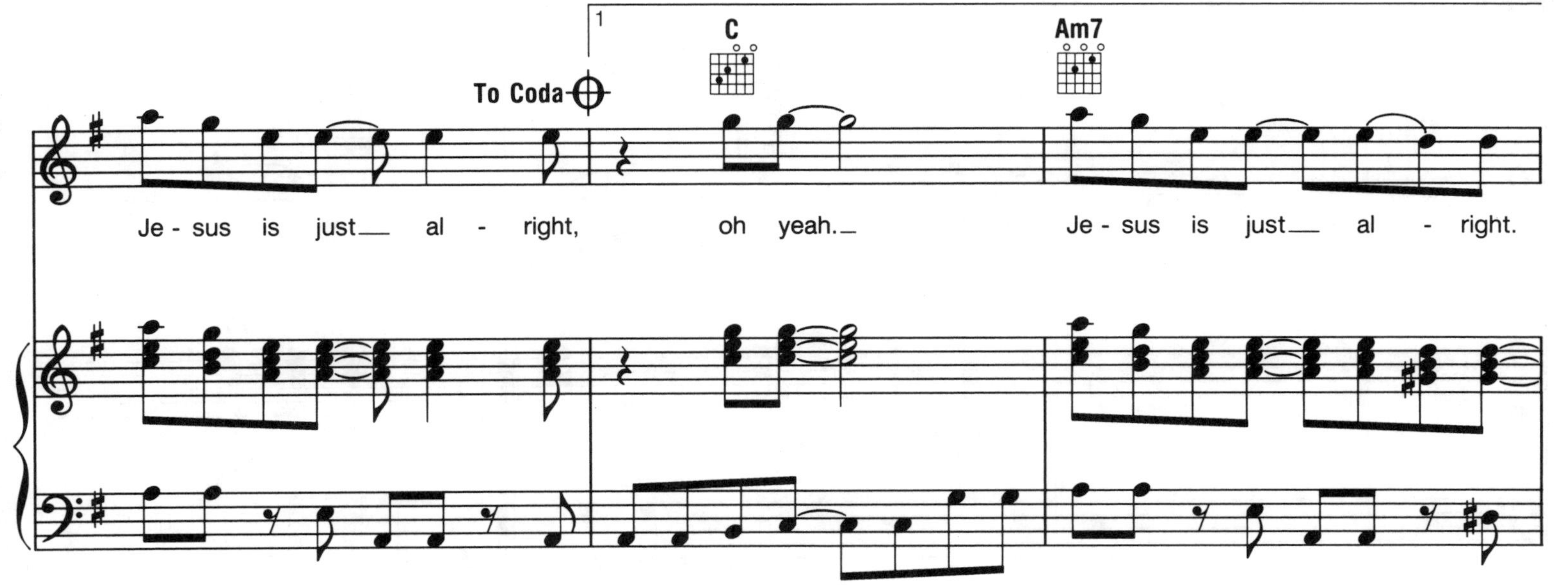

E7#9
F9/E
E7#9
Am
no chord
Oh.
Do do do do do do
do do.
Bm
Am
no chord
Do do do do do do do do.
E7#9
Am
no chord
Do do do do do do do do.
Bm
Am
no chord
Do do do do do do.
E7#9
F9/E
E7#9
a hop - in' and a pray - in'
2
C
oh yeah.

Moderate Jazz Waltz
Am7
D
Am7
D
Am7
D7
Je - sus
he's my
Am7
D7
friend.
Gtr. solo ad lib.

Am7
D
Je - sus,
well he's my
Am7
D7
friend.
Am7
D7
He took me by the hand,
Am7
D
lead me far
from this land.

Am7
D
Je - sus,
he's my
1
Am7
D
D(add9)
friend.
2
Am7
Bright Rock
no chord
Gtr. solo ends
Gtr. solo ad lib. 3rd & 4th times
1-3
4
D.S. al Coda
Gtr. solo ends
CODA
C
oh yeah.

LAY DOWN SALLY

Words and Music by ERIC CLAPTON,
MARCY LEVY and GEORGE TERRY

Bright beat

B♭
There is noth - ing that is wrong in want-ing you to stay
sun ain't near - ly on the rise, and we still got the moon
long to see the morn - ing light col - or - ing your face

E♭
3-
here with me. I
and stars a - bove.
so dream - i - ly. So

Copyright © 1977 by Eric Patrick Clapton and Throat Music Ltd.
All Rights for the U.S. Administered by Unichappell Music Inc.
International Copyright Secured All Rights Reserved

B♭
know you've got some where to go, but won't you make your - self
Un - der - neath the vel - vet skies, love is all that mat -
don't you go and say good - bye; you can lay your wor -
E♭
at home and stay with me? And don't you
ters. Won't you stay with me? And don't you
ries down and stay with me? And don't you
F
F7
B♭
ev - er leave.
ev - er leave.
ev - er leave.
Lay Down Sal -
E♭
ly. and rest you in my arms.

F
B♭
F7
B♭
Don't you think_ you want_ some - one_ to talk_ to?
E♭
Lay Down, Sal - ly; no need to leave_ so soon._
F
B♭
F7
B♭
1
I've been try - ing all_ night long_ just to talk to you._
The
I
2
Repeat and Fade

LET IT BE

Words and Music by JOHN LENNON
and PAUL McCARTNEY

Copyright © 1970 Sony/ATV Songs LLC
All Rights Administered by Sony/ATV Music Publishing, 8 Music Square West, Nashville, TN 37203
International Copyright Secured All Rights Reserved

Am
G
F
C
G
standing right in front of me
Speaking words of wisdom, Let it
F
C/E
Dm7
C
Am
G
be.
Let it be, let it be, let it be,
Let it be, let it be, let it be,
F
C
G
let it be,
let it be,
Whisper words of wisdom, Let it be.
Whisper words of wisdom, Let it be.
F
C/E
Dm7
C
G
And when the broken-hearted people
And when the night is cloudy there is

Am G F C G
liv - ing in the world a - gree There will be an an - swer, Let it
still a light that shines on me Shine un - til to - mor - row. Let it
F C/E Dm7 C G
be. For though they may be part - ed there is
be. I wake up to the sound of mu - sic
Am G F C G
still a chance that they will see There will be an an - swer, Let it
Moth - er Mar - y comes to me Speak - ing words of wis - dom, Let it
F C/E Dm7 C Am G
be. Let it be, let it be, let it be,
be.

F
C
G
let it be,
There will be an an - swer, Let it be.
F
C/E
Dm7
C
G
Am
G
Let it be,
let it be,
let it be,
F
C
G
To Coda
let it be,
Whis - per words of wis - dom, let it be.
There will be an an - swer, let it be.
F
C/E
Dm7
C
F
Em
Dm7
C
B♭
F/A

G F C F C G F C
D.S. al Coda
CODA
F C/E Dm7 C Am G
Let it be, let it be, let it be,
F C G
let it be. Whis-per words of wis - dom, let it be.
F C/E Dm7 C F Em Dm7 C B♭ F/A G F C

LIVIN' ON A PRAYER

Words and Music by JON BON JOVI,
RICHIE SAMBORA and DESMOND CHILD

Copyright © 1986 PolyGram International Publishing, Inc., Bon Jovi Publishing, New Jersey Underground Music Inc., EMI April Music Inc. and Desmobile Music Co., Inc.
All Rights for Desmobile Music Co., Inc. Controlled and Administered by EMI April Music Inc.
International Copyright Secured All Rights Reserved

Em
Em(add F♯)
Em
1. Tom-my used to work on the docks, un-ion's been on strike. He's
2. Tom-my's got his six-string in hock, now he's hold-ing in what he
down on his luck, it's tough, so tough.
used to make it talk. So tough, it's tough.
C
D
3
Em
Gi-na works the din-er all day
Gi-na dreams of run-ning a-way;

Em(addF♯)
Em
3
work-ing for her man. She brings home her pay, for
when she cries in the night, Tom-my whis-pers: ba-by, it's
C
D
love, for love.
O. K. some-day.
C
D
Em
She says we've got to
We've got to
hold on to what we've got. It
f
C
D
Em
C
D
does-n't make a dif-f'rence if we make it or not. We've got each oth-er and

Em
C
D
that's a lot for love. We'll give it a shot.
Chorus:
Em
C
D
G
D7sus4
Wo, we're half - way there. Wo, liv-
Em
C
D
in' on a prayer. Take my hand, we'll make it, I swear.
G
C
D7sus4
1.
Em
Wo, liv - in' on a prayer.

2.
C
Liv - in' on a prayer.
Em C D G C D
(Instrumental)
Em C D
G C Em
Oh, we've got to

C
D
Em
D
C
hold on, ready - y or not, You live for the fight when it's
D
all that you've got.
Repeat and fade
Gm
3fr.
E♭
Fsus4
F
Wo, we're half - way there.
B♭
E♭
F7sus4
Gm
3fr.
E♭
Wo, liv - in' on a prayer. Take my hand and we'll
F
B♭
E♭
F7sus4
make it, I swear. Wo, liv - in' on a prayer.

LONG TALL SALLY

Words and Music by ENOTRIS JOHNSON,
RICHARD PENNIMAN and ROBERT BLACKWELL

Bright rock tempo

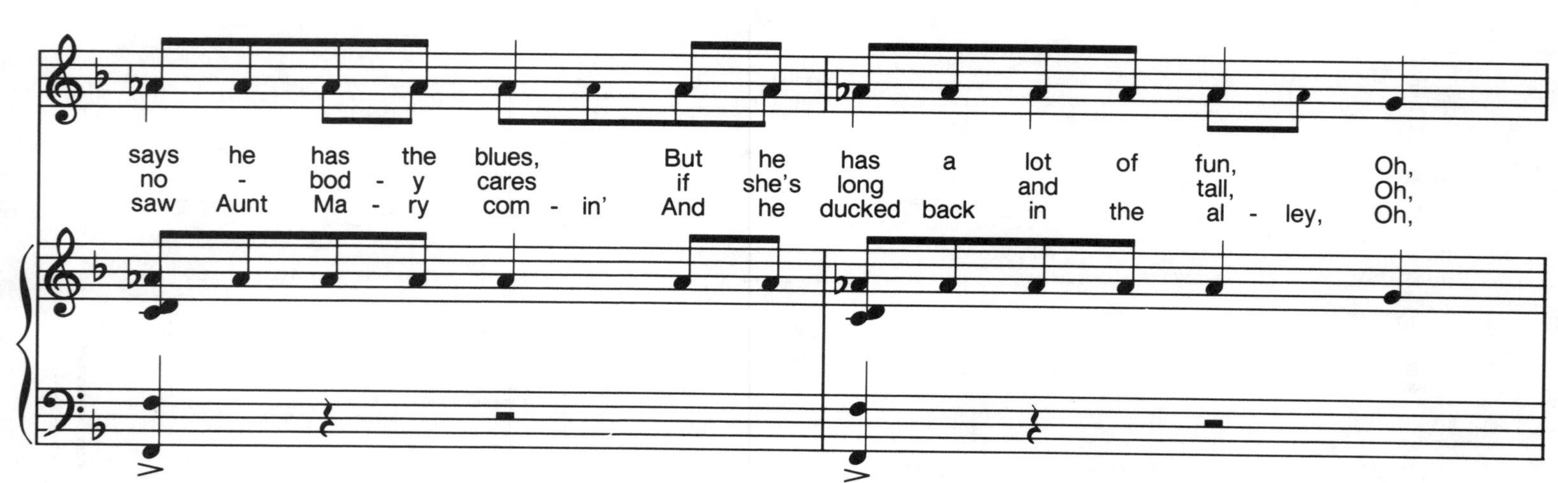

Copyright © 1956 Sony/ATV Songs LLC
Copyright Renewed
All Rights Administered by Sony/ATV Music Publishing, 8 Music Square West, Nashville, TN 37203
International Copyright Secured All Rights Reserved

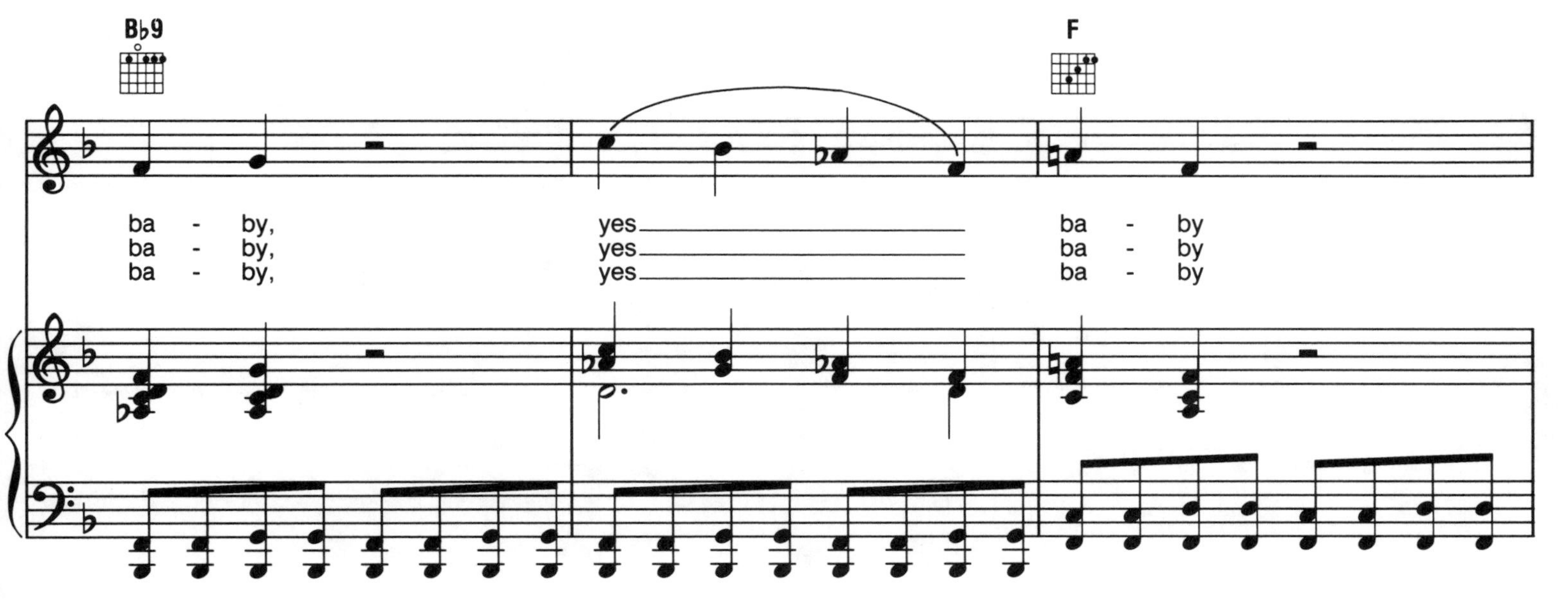
B♭9
F
ba - by,
ba - by,
ba - by,
yes
yes
yes
ba - by
ba - by
ba - by

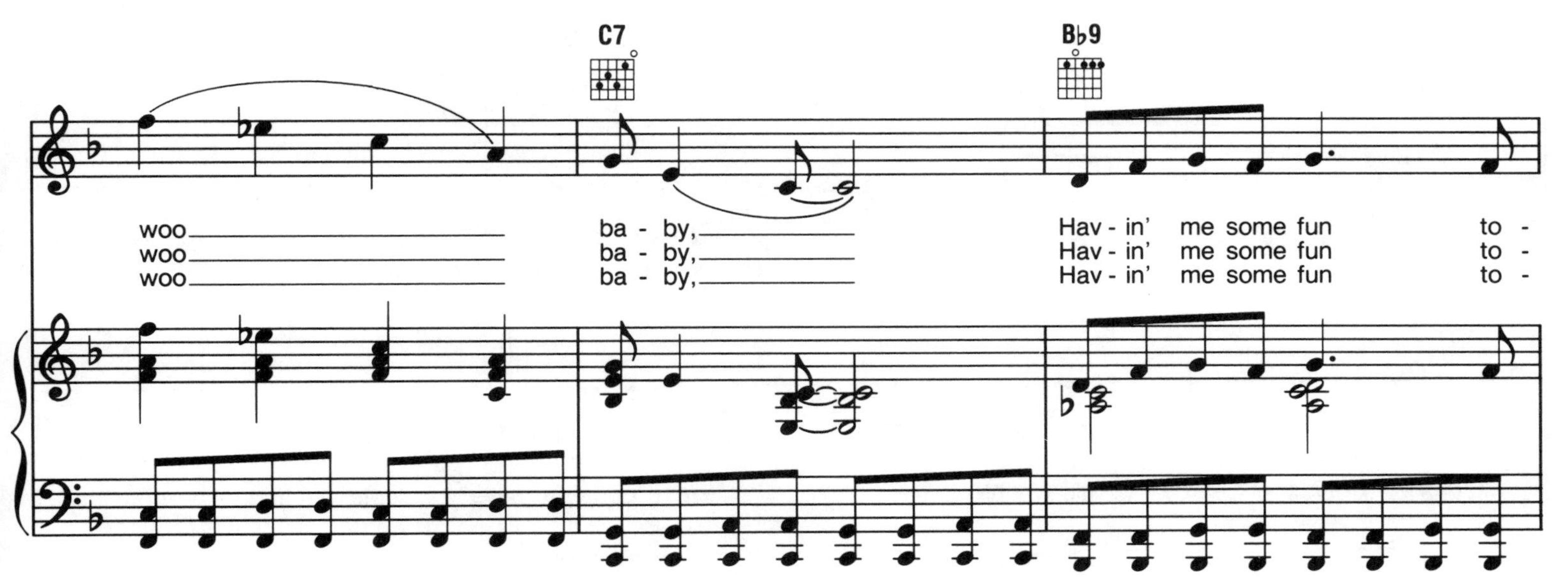
C7
B♭9
woo
woo
woo
ba - by,
ba - by,
ba - by,
Hav - in' me some fun to -
Hav - in' me some fun to -
Hav - in' me some fun to -

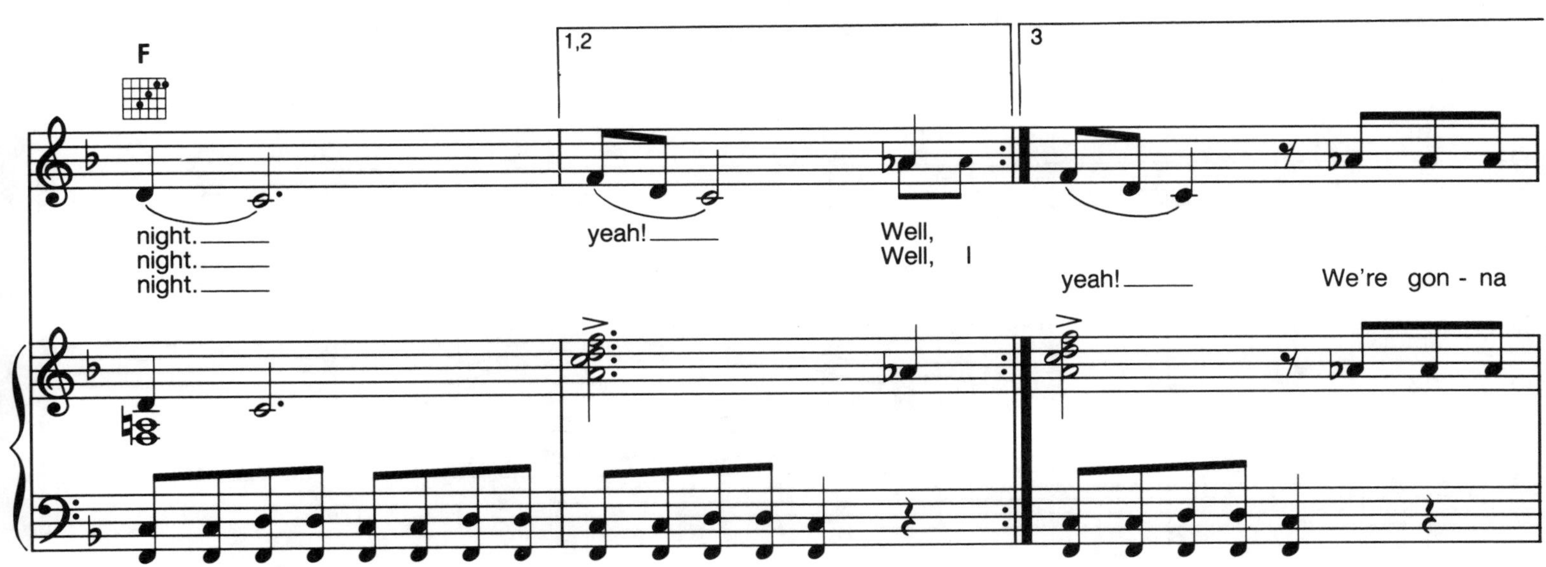
F
1,2
3
night.
night.
night.
yeah!
Well,
Well, I
yeah!
We're gon - na

F
have some fun to - night, Gon - na have some fun to - night
Bb9
woo! We're gon - na have some fun to - night
F
C7
Ev - 'ry - thing will be all right. We're gon - na have some fun, gon - na
Bb9
F
Gm7 F
have some fun to - night!

MAGGIE MAY

Words and Music by ROD STEWART
and MARTIN QUITTENTON

Moderately bright

mf

A G D

Wake up, Mag-gie, I think I got some-thing to say to you: It's

A G D

late Sep - tem-ber and I real - ly should be back at school. I

G D G A

know I keep you a - mused, but I feel I'm be - ing used, Oh,

Copyright © 1971 by Unichappell Music Inc., Rod Stewart and Windswept Pacific Entertainment Co. d/b/a Full Keel Music Co.
All Rights for Rod Stewart Controlled and Administered by EMI April Music Inc.
International Copyright Secured All Rights Reserved

Em
F#m
Em7
Mag - gie, I could - n't have tried any - y more. You
Em
A
Em
A
lured me a - way from home, just to save you from be - ing a - lone. You
Em
A
D
stole my heart and that's what real - ly hurts. The
A
G
D
morn - ing sun, when it's in your face, real - ly shows your age, But
A
G
D
G
that don't wor - ry me none in my eyes you're ev - 'ry - thing. I laughed at all of your

2. You lured me away from home, just to save you from being alone.
You stole my soul, that's a pain I can do without.
All I needed was a friend to lend a guiding hand.
But you turned into a lover, and, Mother, what a lover! You wore me out.
All you did was wreck my bed, and in the morning kick me in the head.
Oh, Maggie, I couldn't have tried any more.

3. You lured me away from home, 'cause you didn't want to be alone.
You stole my heart, I couldn't leave you if I tried.
I suppose I could collect my books and get back to school.
Or steal my Daddy's cue and make a living out of playing pool,
Or find myself a rock and roll band that needs a helpin' hand.
Oh, Maggie, I wish I'd never seen your face. **(To Coda)**

LOVE IS A BATTLEFIELD

Words and Music by MIKE CHAPMAN
and HOLLY KNIGHT

Copyright © 1983 by BMG Songs, Inc. and Mike Chapman Enterprises, Inc.
International Copyright Secured All Rights Reserved

Dm
C
Am
B♭
Love is a bat - tle - field.
Dm
C
Am
B♭
Dm
C
We are__ strong.
Am
B♭
Dm
C
Am
B♭
No one can tell us we're wrong,__
search - ing__ our hearts for__ so
Dm
C
Am
B♭
long;______
both of us__ know-ing__

Dm
love is a bat - tle - field.
C/D
B♭/D
Dm
You're beg - ging me to go, then
los - ing con - trol, will you
C
B♭maj7
Gm
making me stay.
turn me a - way,
Why do you hurt me so bad?
or touch me deep in - side?
It would
And when

Dm
C
help me to know do I stand in your way,
all this gets old, will it still feel the same?
Bbmaj7
Gm
Dm
or am I the best thing you've had? Be-lieve me, be-lieve me, I
There's no way this will die. But if we get much clos-er I
C
Bb
Gm
can't tell you why, but I'm trapped by your love and I'm chained to your side.
could lose con-trol and if your heart sur-rend-ers you'll need me to hold.
Dm
C
We are young.

Am
Bb
Dm
C
Am
Bb
Heart-ache to heart-ache we stand;
no prom - is - es, no de-mands.
Dm
C
Am
Bb
Dm
C
Love is a bat - tle-field.
Am
Bb
Dm
C
Am
Bb
We are strong.
We are strong.
No one can tell us we're wrong,
Dm
C
Am
Bb
search - ing our hearts for so

Dm
C
Am
B♭
long; ___
both of us __ know-ing __
To Coda
Dm
love is a bat - tle - field.
C/D
D.S. al Coda
When I'm
CODA
Dm
C/D
B♭/D
Repeat and Fade

MAGIC CARPET RIDE

Words and Music by JOHN KAY
and RUSHTON MOREVE

© Copyright 1968 by MCA - DUCHESS MUSIC CORPORATION and KINGS ROAD MUSIC
Copyright Renewed
All Rights Controlled and Administered by MCA - DUCHESS MUSIC CORPORATION
International Copyright Secured All Rights Reserved
MCA Music Publishing

D C G D C G
we can find. Oh, why don't you come with me lit - tle girl
D C G D C G D C G
on a mag - ic car - pet ride. Well, you don't know what we can see.
D C G D C G
Why don't you tell your dreams to me, fan - tas - y will set you free. Close your eyes girl,
B♭ C G(no3rd)
To Coda
look in - side girl, let the sound take you a - way.

D
C
G
Last night I owned Al - lad - in's lamp
and so I wished that I could stay.
Be - fore the thing could an - swer me,
some-one came and took the lamp a - way.
I looked a - round
a lous-y can - dle is all I found. Well,
D.S. al Coda
CODA
G(no3rd)
way.

MY GENERATION

Words and Music by
PETER TOWNSHEND

© Copyright 1965 (Renewed) Fabulous Music Ltd., London, England
TRO - Devon Music, Inc., New York, controls all publication rights for the U.S.A. and Canada
International Copyright Secured
All Rights Reserved Including Public Performance For Profit
Used by Permission

F
Eb
Bb
Hope I die be-fore I get old.
This is my gen-er-
[Talk-in' 'bout my gen-er-a-tion]
a-tion,
This is my gen-er-a-tion, ba-by.
Why don't you all fade a-way?
[Talk-in' 'bout my gen-er-a-tion]
Don't try and dig what we all say.
I'm
[Talk-in' 'bout my gen-er-a-tion]

F
Eb
F
Bb
Eb
not tryin' to cause a big sen - sa - tion. I'm just
[Talk - in' 'bout my gen - er - a - tion]
F
Eb
F
Bb
Eb
talk - in' 'bout my gen - er - a - tion.
This is my gen-er-
[Talk - in' 'bout my gen - er - a - tion]
F
Eb
F
Eb
a - tion,
This is my gen - er - a - tion, ba - by.
1.
2.
NC
F
Eb6
F

NA NA HEY HEY KISS HIM GOODBYE

Words and Music by ARTHUR FRASHUER DALE,
PAUL ROGER LEKA and GARY CARLA

Copyright © 1969 by Unichappell Music Inc.
Copyright Renewed
International Copyright Secured All Rights Reserved

Bb
A7
Dm7
G7
He might be thrill - ing ba - by, but, my love's so dog - gone will - ing so
F
Bb
Bbm
C6
F
kiss him, go on and kiss him good - bye. Na na
Ab
1
Eb
F
C7
2
Eb
F
C7
na na, Hey hey, hey, good - bye. Na na hey, hey good - bye. Na na
Repeat and Fade
F
Ab
Eb
F
C7
na na na na na na, Hey hey hey, good - bye. Na na

OH, PRETTY WOMAN

Words and Music by ROY ORBISON
and BILL DEES

Copyright © 1964 (Renewed 1992) BARBARA ORBISON MUSIC COMPANY, ORBI-LEE MUSIC, R-KEY DARKUS MUSIC and ACUFF-ROSE MUSIC, INC.
International Copyright Secured All Rights Reserved

D
E7
wom - an
wom - an
I don't be - lieve you, you're not the
that you look love - ly as can
truth No one could look as good as
be Are you lone - ly just like
you.
me?
N.C.
Mer - cy.
1
E7
Pret - ty
2
E7

Dm
G7
Pret - ty wom - an stop a - while,
C
Am
Dm
Pret - ty wom - an talk a - while,
Pret - ty wom - an
G7
C
give your smile to me.
Dm
G7
C
Pret - ty wom - an yeah, yeah, yeah,
Pret - ty wom - an

Am
Dm
look my way,
Pret - ty wom - an
G7
C
A7
say you'll stay with me.
'Cause I
F♯m
Dm
E7
need you
I'll treat you right.
A
F♯m
Dm
Come with me ba - by.
Be mine to -

E7
night.
A
F♯m
Pret - ty wom - an don't walk on by, Pret - ty
A
F♯m
wom - an don't make me cry, Pret - ty
D
E7
wom - an don't walk a - way.

Hey,
O. K.
If that's the way it must be O. K.
I guess I'll go on home, it's late
There'll be to-
mor - row night
but wait!
N.C.
What do I see?

E7
Is she walk - ing back to -
me?
Yeah, she's
walk - ing back to me!
A
Oh,
Pret - ty wom - an.

ROCKIN' ROBIN

Words and Music by
J. THOMAS

Bright Rock Tempo
F6
C7
F6
F
1.,3. He rocks in the tree - top, all the day long,
2. Ev - 'ry lit - tle swal-low, ev - 'ry chick - a - dee,
Hop - pin' and a - bop - pin' and a - sing - in' his song. All the lit - tle birds on
Ev - 'ry lit - tle bird in the tall oak tree. The wise old owl, the
Jay - bird street, love to hear the rob - in go "Tweet, tweet, tweet."
big black crow, flap their wings, sing - in' "Go bird, go."
Rock - in'

© 1958 Recordo Music Publishers
Copyright Renewed
All Rights Reserved

B♭9
F
Rob - in, __
Rock - in' Rob - in,
C7
B♭9
To Coda
Blow, Rock - in' Rob - in, 'cause we're real - ly gon - na rock to - night. _
1 F
B♭9
F
2 F
B♭9
F
B♭
A pret - ty lit - tle ra - ven at the bird band - stand,

F
taught him how to do the bop and it was grand. They
B♭
start - ed go - in' stead - y, and bless my soul, He
C7
D.S. al Coda
out - bopped the buz - zard and the o - ri - ole. He
CODA
F
B♭
F
ff

PRIDE
(In the Name of Love)

Lyrics by BONO
Music by U2

Copyright © 1984 PolyGram International Music Publishing B.V.
All Rights for the United States and Canada Administered by PolyGram International Publishing, Inc.
International Copyright Secured All Rights Reserved

B♭(add9)
Gm11
Csus
One man come in the name
One man caught on a barbed
F(add9)
B♭(add9)
Gm11
of love, one man come and go.
wire fence, one man he re - sist.
Csus
F(add9)
B♭(add9)
One man come he to jus - ti - fy, one man to o - ver - throw.
One man washed on an emp - ty beach, one man be-trayed with a
Gm11
C
F
kiss.
In the name of love, what more

B♭
G
C
in the name of love? In the name of love,
F
B♭
what more in the name of love?
1 G
2 G
C
In the name of love,
F
B♭
G
what more in the name of love, in the name

C
F
B♭
of love?
What more
in the name of,
G
no chord
in the name of love?

Csus
F(add9)
B♭(add9)
Gm11
Csus
Ooh
ooh
F(add9)
B♭(add9)
Gm11
ooh
ooh.

Csus
F(add9)
B♭(add9)
Ear - ly morn-ing, A - pril four, a shot rings out in the
Gm11
Csus
F(add9)
Mem - phis sky. Free at last, they took your life. They
B♭(add9)
Gm11
C
could not take your pride. In the name of love,
F
B♭
G
Repeat ad lib. and Fade
what more in the name of love? In the name

RIKKI DON'T LOSE THAT NUMBER

Words and Music by WALTER BECKER
and DONALD FAGEN

Moderately
no chord
mf
D
A
E
We hear you're leav - ing, that's O. K.
I have a friend in town, he's heard your name.
3
D
A
I thought our lit - tle wild time had just be -
We can go out driv - ing on Slow Hand
E
C♯
B
D
gun.
Row.
I guess you kind of
We could stay in

© Copyright 1974 by MCA MUSIC PUBLISHING, A Division of UNIVERSAL STUDIOS, INC.
International Copyright Secured All Rights Reserved
MCA Music Publishing

A
E
scared your - self, you turn and run.
side and play games I don't know.
F♯m7
A
But if you have a change of heart,
And you could have a change of heart.
no chord
E
Rik - ki, don't lose that num - ber; you don't wan - na
G
call no - bod - y else.
A
Send it off in a

G
D
let - ter to your - self.
C
Em
Rik - ki, don't lose that num - ber; it's the on - ly one you own.
C
D
A
You might use it if you feel bet - ter
no chord
To Coda
when you get home.

Amaj7
G#m7
You tell your - self you're not my kind,
Amaj7
C#m7
F#m7
but you don't e - ven know your mind.
And you could have a
A
D.S. al Coda
change of heart.
CODA
E
Rik - ki, don't lose that num -
ber,
Rik - ki, don't lose that num - ber.
Rik - ki, don't lose that num - ber.

ROCK AROUND THE CLOCK

Words and Music by MAX C. FREEDMAN
and JIMMY DeKNIGHT

Copyright © 1953 Myers Music Inc. and Capano Music
Copyright Renewed 1981
All Rights on behalf of Myers Music Inc. Administered by Sony/ATV Music Publishing, 8 Music Square West, Nashville, TN 37203
International Copyright Secured All Rights Reserved

F7
B♭9
clock strikes one, We're gon-na rock a-round the clock to-night, We're gon-na
yell for more, We're gon-na rock a-round the clock to-night, We're gon-na
sev-enth heav'n, We're gon-na rock a-round the clock to-night, We're gon-na
so will you, We're gon-na rock a-round the clock to-night, We're gon-na
clock a-gain, We're gon-na rock a-round the clock to-night, We're gon-na
F
G7
rock, rock, rock, 'til broad day-light, We're gon-na rock, gon-na rock a-round
Gm7
C7♯5
C9sus
1-4
F
the clock to-night.
2. When the
3. When the
4. When it's
5. When the
5
F

RUNAWAY

Words and Music by DEL SHANNON
and MAX CROOK

© 1961 Mole Hole Music and Bug Music
Copyright Renewed
All Rights Administered by Bug Music
International Copyright Secured All Rights Reserved

D♭
C7
geth - er while our hearts _ were young.
F
Dm
I'm a - walk - in' in the rain. _ Tears are fall - in' and I feel a pain, _
F
Dm
a - wish - in' you were here by me _ To end this mis - er - y. _ And I
F
Dm
won - der, wo - wo - wo - wo - won - der _

F
Dm
why, why - why - why - why - why she run - a - way, And I
F
C7
C7
C7sus
won - der where she will stay, my lit - tle
F
B♭
1 F
Run - a - way, run - run - run - run - Run - a - way.
C7
2 F
Run - a - way.

SHAKE, RATTLE AND ROLL

Words and Music by
CHARLES CALHOUN

Moderately Bright
mf

VERSE
C6
Get out ___ from that kitch - en and rat - tle those pots and pans, ___

C7
F9
C6
Get out ___ from that kitch - en and rat - tle those pots and pans. ___

Copyright © 1954 by Unichappell Music Inc.
Copyright Renewed
International Copyright Secured All Rights Reserved

Cdim
Dm7
G9
C6
Well, roll my break-fast, 'cause I'm a hun-gry man.
CHORUS
C6
Shake Rat-tle and Roll,
Shake rat-tle and roll,
C7
F9
C6
Shake rat-tle and roll,
Shake rat-tle and roll;
Cdim
Dm7
G7
You nev-er do noth-in' to save your dog-gone

1
C6
to 2nd Verse
soul.
2
C6
to 3rd Verse
soul.
3
C6
Fine
soul.
Verse 2
C6
Wear - in' those dress - es, your hair done up so right,
C7
F9
Wear - in' those dress - es, your
C6
Cdim
hair done up so right;
You

Dm7
G9
C6
D.S. 2nd ending
look so warm, but your heart is cold as ice.
Verse 3
C6
I'm like a one-eyed cat, peep-in' in a sea-food store,
C7
F9
I'm like a one-eyed cat,
C6
Cdim
Dm7
peep-in' in a sea-food store; I can look at you, tell you

Verse 4
C7
C6
C6
don't love me no more.
I be -
lieve you're do - in' me wrong __ and now I know, _
C7
I be -
F9
C6
Cdim
lieve you're do - in' me wrong _ and now I know; _
The
Dm7
G7
C6
D.S. al Fine
(3rd ending)
more I work, the fast - er my mon - ey goes. ____

(She's) SOME KIND OF WONDERFUL

Words and Music by
JOHN ELLISON

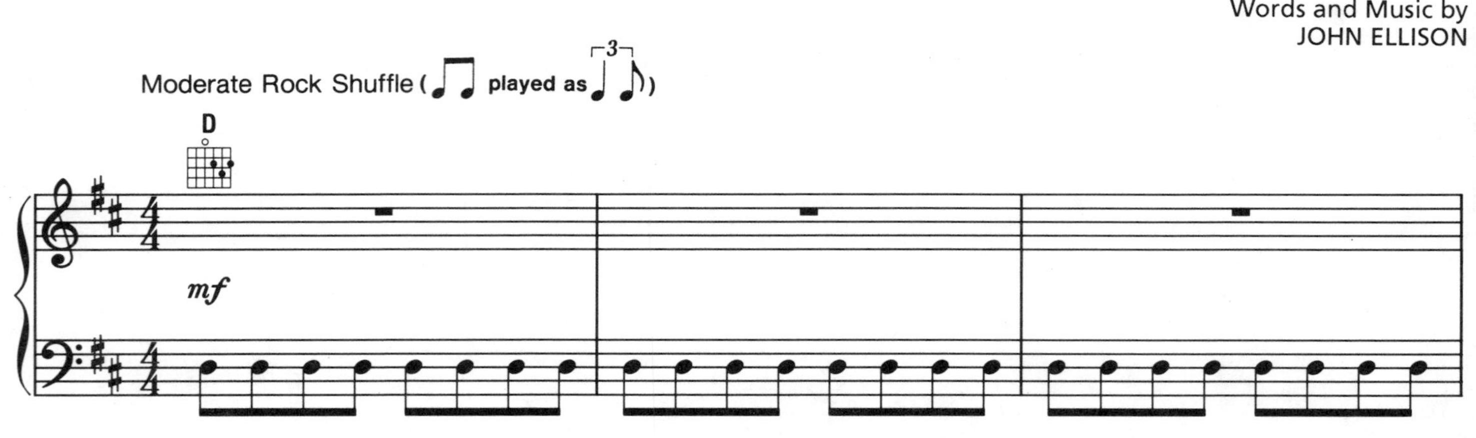

Copyright © 1967 by Dandelion Music Company
Copyright Renewed
International Copyright Secured All Rights Reserved

man could want. I got more than I could ask
es me my heart be - comes filled with de -
3
3

G
for. I, I don't have to
sire. When she wraps her lov - in' arms a - round

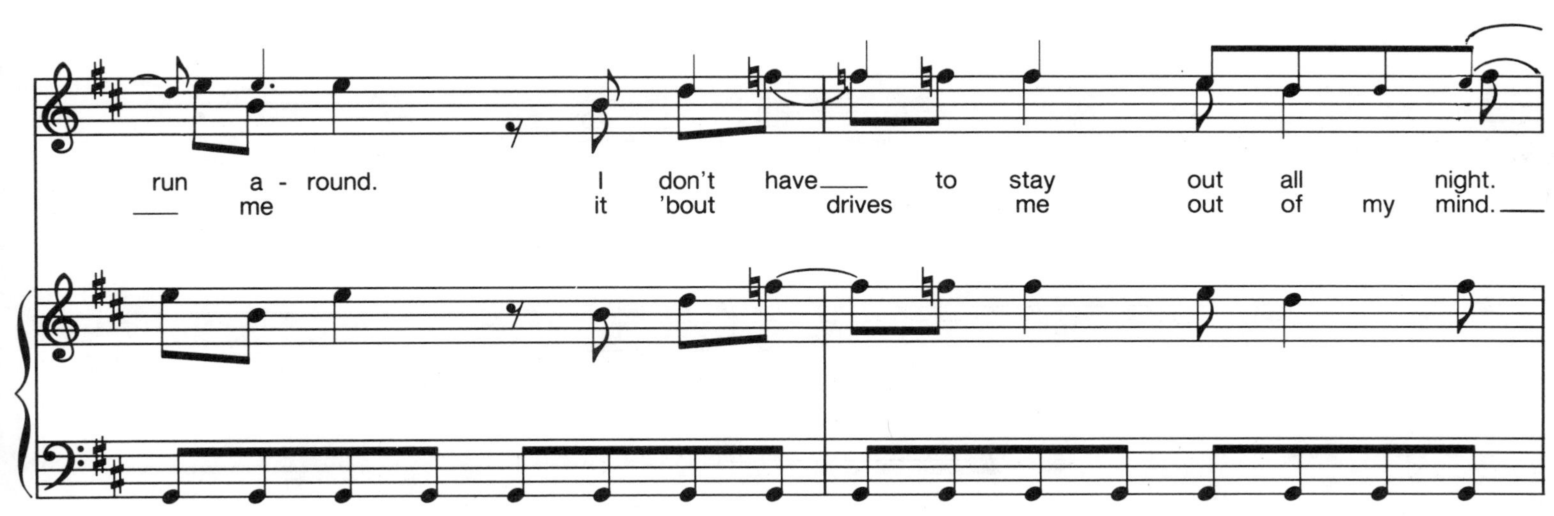
run a - round. I don't have to stay out all night.
me it 'bout drives me out of my mind.

D
'Cause I got me a sweet a sweet lov - in'
Yeah, when my ba - by kiss -
wo - man and she knows just how to treat me right.
es me chills run up and down my spine.
A
Well my ba - by, she's al - right.

G
Well, my ba - by she's clean out of
D
sight. Don't you know that she's, know that she is, she's some kind of
G
won - der - ful.
D
She's some kind of
G
won - der - ful. Yeah, she is, she's,
D
she's some kind of

G
D
won - der - ful. Yeah, yeah yeah yeah.
When I hold
D
yeah.
Now is there an - y - bod - y
got a sweet lit - tle wo - man like mine?
There's got to be some - bod - y got

3
a, got a sweet___ lit - tle wo - man like mine. Yeah.
3
Now can I get a wit - ness? Can I get a
Bm
wit - ness? Well, can I get a
D
Bm
wit - ness? Can I get a wit - ness?

D
Can I get a wit - ness?
Can I get a
Bm
wit - ness
I'm talk - in', talk - in' 'bout my
D
G
ba - by.
Talk - in' 'bout my
She's some kind of won - der - ful.
ba - by.
D
Repeat ad lib. and Fade
Talk - in' 'bout my
3
She's some kind of won - der - ful.
3

SUMMER IN THE CITY

Words and Music by JOHN SEBASTIAN, STEVE BOONE and MARK SEBASTIAN

Moderately, with a steady beat

mf

Cm Cm/B♭ Cm/A Csus2/A♭ G

Hot town, summer in the city, back o' my neck getting dirty and gritty.
Cool town, evenin' in the city, dressed so fine and-a lookin' so pretty.
Instrumental to Fade

Cm Cm/B♭ Cm/A Csus2/A♭ G

Been down, isn't it a pity. Doesn't seem to be a shadow in the city.
Cool cat, lookin' for a kitty. Gonna look in ev'ry corner of the city.

G7/B Cm C

All around, people lookin' half dead, Walkin' on the sidewalk hotter than a match, yeah.
Till I'm wheezin' like a bus stop. Runnin' up the stairs, gonna meet you on the rooftop.

Copyright © 1966 by Alley Music Corp., Trio Music Co., Inc. and Mark Sebastian
Copyright Renewed
International Copyright Secured All Rights Reserved
Used by Permission

F
Bb
But at night it's a dif - f'rent world,
F
Bb
F
Bb
Go out and find a girl.
Come on, come on and dance all night,
F
Bb
Dm
G
de - spite the heat it - 'll be al - right,
And babe, don't you know it's a pit - y, The
Dm
G
Dm
G
days can't be like the nights, In the sum - mer in the cit - y, In the

1
Dm
G
2
Dm
G
sum - mer in the cit - y.
sum - mer in the cit - y.
Cm
Ab7
(Instrumental)
Cm
Ab7
Cm
Cm/Bb
D.S. and Fade
(Instrumental)
Cm/A
Csus2/Ab
G
Cm
Cm/Bb
Cm/A
Csus2/Ab
G

SPINNING WHEEL

Words and Music by
DAVID CLAYTON THOMAS

© 1968 (Renewed 1996) EMI BLACKWOOD MUSIC INC. and BAY MUSIC LTD.
All Rights Controlled and Administered by EMI BLACKWOOD MUSIC INC.
All Rights Reserved International Copyright Secured Used by Permission

E7
A7
D7
G
E7
A7
You got no mon - ey, you got no home, spin - ning wheel
D7
G
E7
A7
D7
G
all a - lone, talk - in' 'bout your trou - bles and you, you nev - er learn,
D7
N.C.
D7♯9
ride a paint - ed po - ny, let the spin - ning wheel turn.
C
B♭
Did you find your di - rect - ing sign on the

A♭
4 fr
G
C
straight and nar - row high - way.
Would you mind a re -
B♭
A♭
4 fr
G
flect - ing sign? Just let it shine with - in your mind, and
A♭
4 fr
B♭
C
show you the col - ors that are real.
D9
4 fr

E7
A7
D7
G
Some - one is wait - ing just for you, spin - ning wheel
spin - ning true. Drop all your trou - bles by the riv - er - side,
D7
N.C.
D7#9
catch a paint - ed po - ny on the spin - ning wheel ride.
Repeat and Fade

STAY

Words and Music by
MAURICE WILLIAMS

© 1960 (Renewed) CHERIO CORP.
All Rights Reserved

Eb
F7
Bb
Gm
Eb
F7
Could we have an - oth - er dance dear, just - a one more,
Gm
Tacet
Bb
Gm
one more time? Oh, won't you stay
Eb
F7
Bb
Gm
Eb
F7
just a lit - tle bit long - er? Please let me
Bb
Gm
Eb
F7
Bb
3
dance. Please say that you will.

SUNSHINE OF YOUR LOVE

Words and Music by JACK BRUCE,
PETE BROWN and ERIC CLAPTON

Moderate Rock
mf
D
C
D
It's get - ting near dawn_ when
with you my love,_ The
lights close their tired_ eyes,_ I'll soon be with you,_ my love,_
light's shin - ing through_ on you,_ Yes, I'm with you, my love,_
to give you my dawn_ sur - prise,_ I'll
It's the morn - ing and just_ we two,_ I'll

Copyright © 1968, 1973 by Dratleaf Ltd.
Copyright Renewed
All Rights Administered by Unichappell Music Inc.
International Copyright Secured All Rights Reserved

G
F
G
F
G
be with you, dar - ling, soon,
I'll be with you when the stars
stay with you, dar - ling, now,
I'll stay with you 'til my seeds
To Coda
D
C
D
start fall - ing.
are dried up.
C
D
A
I've been wait-
C
G
A
C
G
- ing so long
to be where I'm go - ing

A
C
G
A
In the sun - shine of your love.
D
C
D
D.S. al Coda
I'm
CODA
D
C
D
C
D
A
C
G
I've been wait - ing so long,

A
C
G
A
I've been wait - ing so long.
I've been wait - ing so long
C
G
A
C
G
to be where I'm go - ing
A
C
G
A
In the sun - shine of your love.

TAKIN' CARE OF BUSINESS

Words and Music by
RANDY BACHMAN

Copyright © 1974 Sony/ATV Songs LLC
All Rights Administered by Sony/ATV Music Publishing, 8 Music Square West, Nashville, TN 37203
International Copyright Secured All Rights Reserved

C7
ci - ty. There's a whis - tle up a - bove and peo - ple
mel - low. Get a sec - ond hand gui - tar chanc - es

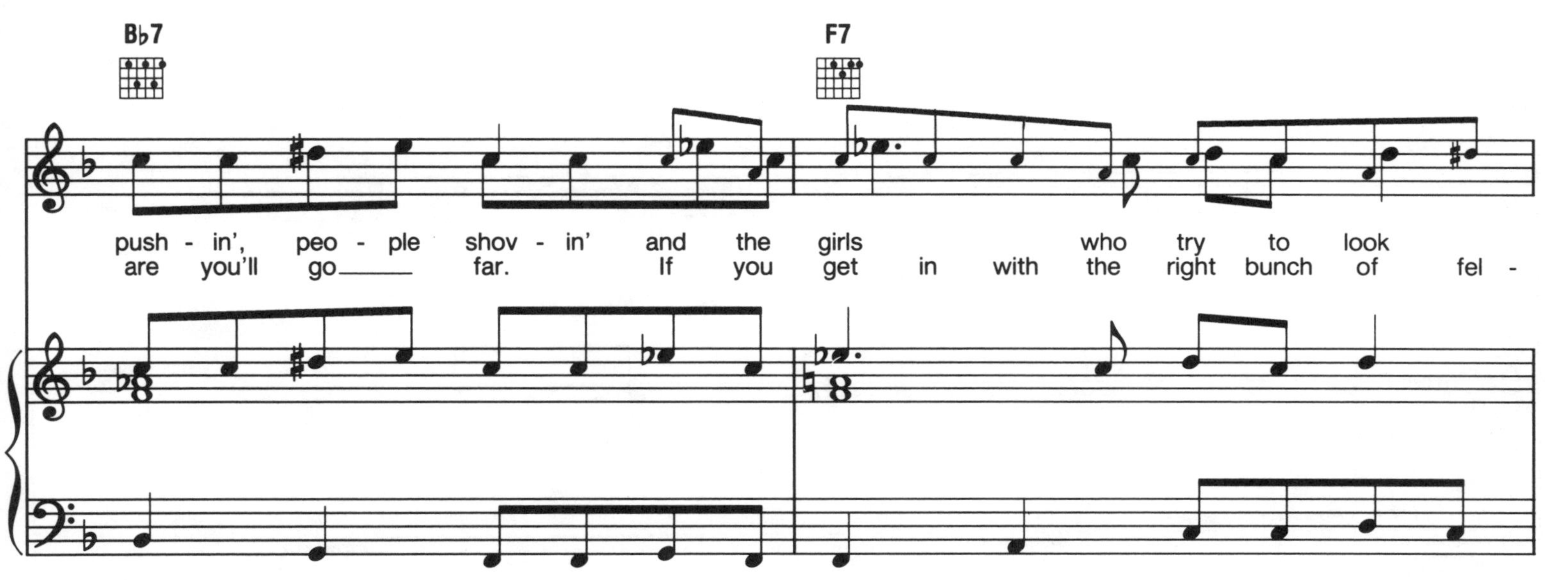
B♭7
F7
push - in', peo - ple shov - in' and the girls who try to look
are you'll go far. If you get in with the right bunch of fel -

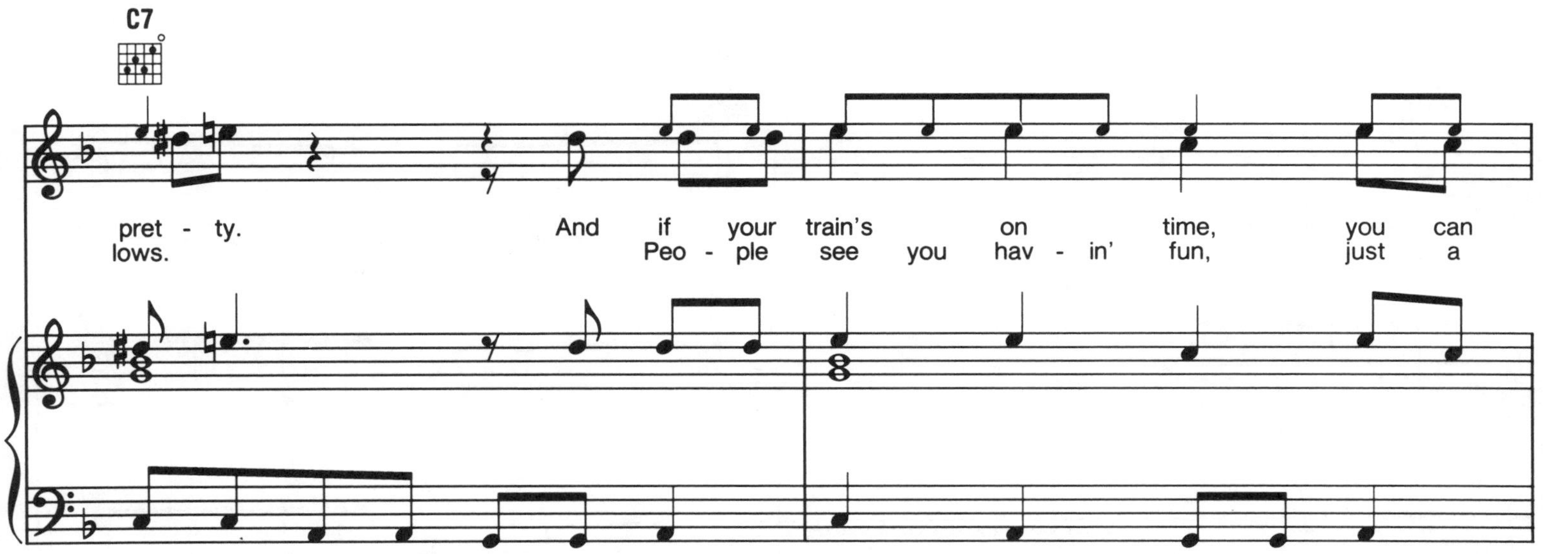
C7
pret - ty. And if your train's on time, you can
lows. Peo - ple see you hav - in' fun, just a

B♭7
F7
get to work by nine, and start your slav - in' job to get your
ly - in' in the sun. Tell them that you like it this way.

C7
pay. If you ev - er get an - noyed look at
It's the work that we a - void and we're

B♭7
F7
me, I'm self em - ployed, I love to work at noth - in' all day.
all self em - ployed. We like to work at noth - in' all day.

C7
And I've been
And we been
tak - in' care of busi - ness,
B♭7
F7
ev - 'ry day.
Tak - in' care of busi - ness,
C7
ev - 'ry way.
I've
We
I've
been tak - in' care of busi - ness.
B♭7
F7
To Coda
It's all mine.
Tak - in' care of busi - ness and

C7
work - in' o - ver - time, work - out.
work - in' o - ver - time.
B♭7
F7
C7
B♭7
F7
1 C7
There's work
2 C7

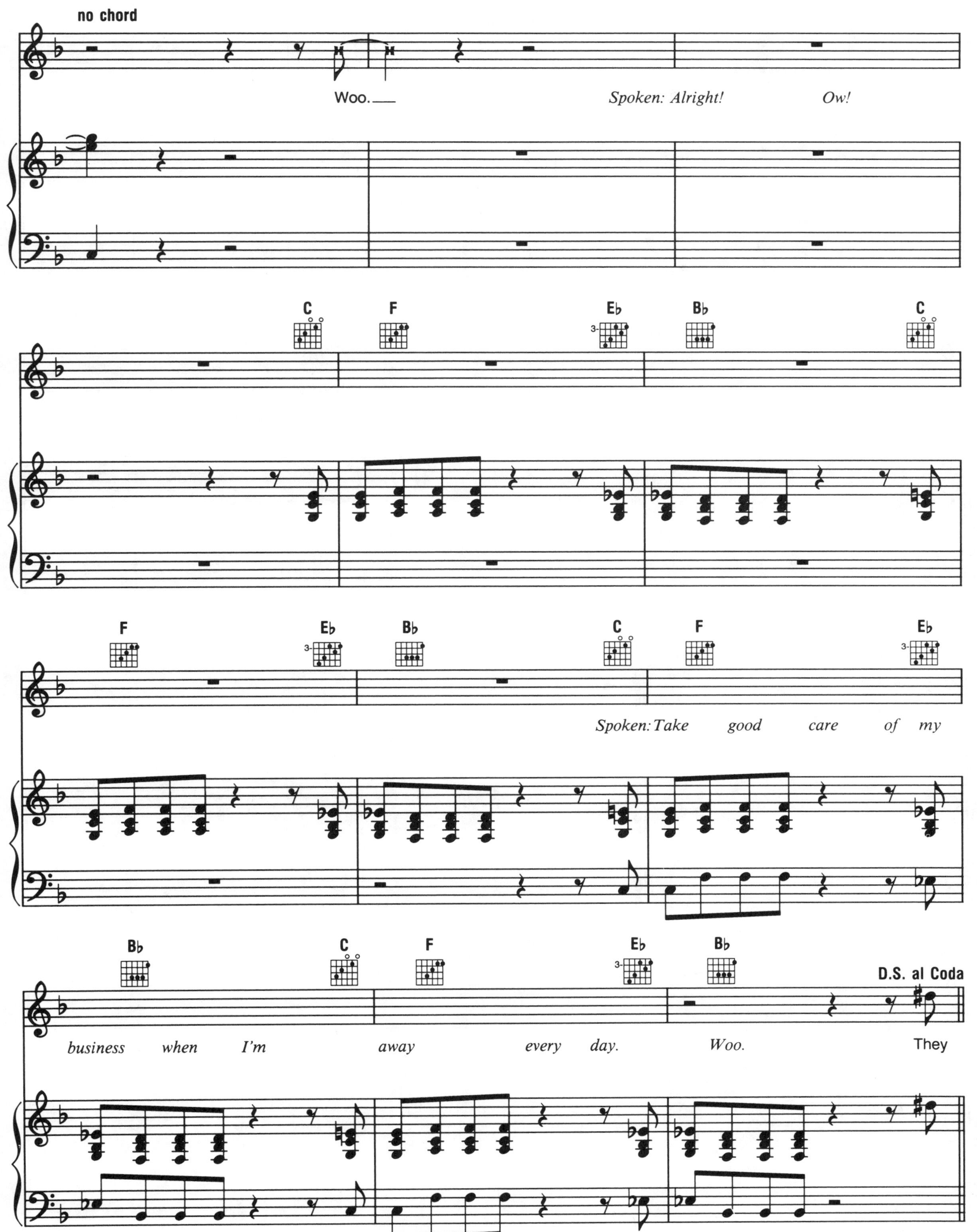
no chord
Woo.
Spoken: Alright!
Ow!
C
F
E♭
B♭
C
F
E♭
B♭
C
F
E♭
Spoken: Take good care of my
B♭
C
F
E♭
B♭
D.S. al Coda
business when I'm away every day.
Woo.
They

CODA
C7
no chord
work - in' o - ver - time.
Tak - in' care of busi - ness.
1-3
4
C(no3rd)
B♭(no3rd)
Tak–
Tak - in' care of busi - ness,
F(no3rd)
C(no3rd)
ev - 'ry day.
Tak - in' care of busi - ness,

C(no3rd)
Bb(no3rd)
F(no3rd)
ev - 'ry way. Tak - in' care of busi - ness. It's all mine. Tak -
C(no3rd)
in' care of busi - ness and work - in' o - ver - time.
C7
Bb7
F7
Tak - in' care of busi - ness. Tak - in' care of busi - ness.
C7
Bb7
Repeat and Fade
We been tak - in' care of busi - ness. We been tak -

TUTTI FRUTTI

Words and Music by LITTLE RICHARD PENNIMAN
and DOROTHY LA BOSTRIE

Copyright © 1955, 1956 Sony/ATV Songs LLC
Copyright Renewed
All Rights Administered by Sony/ATV Music Publishing, 8 Music Square West, Nashville, TN 37203
International Copyright Secured All Rights Reserved

G7
rut - ti,
Tut - ti
Frut - ti
au
rut - ti,
Tut - ti
D9
C9
Frut - ti
au
rut - ti,
A -
G
Am7
G
Am7
G
bop - bop a - loom - op a - lop bop boom! I got a
gal, her name's Sue, She knows just what to do,
gal, her name's Dai - sy, She al - most drives me cra -

G7
C7
I got a gal, her name's Sue, She
-zy. I got a gal, her name's Dai - sy, She
G
C7
G
knows just what to do.
al - most drives me cra - zy.
I've
She's a
been to the east, I've been to the west, But
real gone cook - ie, yes - sir - ree, But
C7
she's the gal I love the best.
pret - ty lit - tle Su - zy's the gal for me.
Tut - ti Frut - ti au

G
rut - ti, Tut - ti Frut - ti au rut - ti, Tut - ti
C7
G
Frut - ti au rut - ti, Tut - ti Frut - ti au
D9
C9
rut - ti, Tut - ti Frut - ti au rut - ti, A -
G
Am7
1
2
bop - bop a - loom - op a - lop bop boom! (2) I got a lop bop boom!

THE TWIST

Words and Music by
HANK BALLARD

Copyright © 1959 by Fort Knox Music Inc. and Trio Music Co., Inc.
Copyright Renewed
International Copyright Secured All Rights Reserved
Used by Permission

C7
G
G7
and go like this:
tear the house down.
and she knows how to Twist.
Ee oh
Ee oh Twist,
Ee oh
C7
ba - by, ba - by, Twist, ('round and a - round and a - round and a)- Just,
G
D7
just like this, ('round and a - round) Come on, lit - tle miss,
C7
G
1,2
3
and do The Twist. ('round and a - round.) While Dad - dy is
You should round.)

TWIST AND SHOUT

Words and Music by BERT RUSSELL
and PHIL MEDLEY

© 1960 (Renewed 1988) SCREEN GEMS-EMI MUSIC INC., UNICHAPPELL MUSIC INC. and SLOOPY II, INC.
All Rights for UNICHAPPELL MUSIC INC. in the U.S. Controlled and Administered by SCREEN GEMS-EMI MUSIC INC.
All Rights outside the U.S. Controlled and Administered by SCREEN GEMS-EMI MUSIC INC.
All Rights Reserved International Copyright Secured Used by Permission

D G A7 D G
ba - by now, Come on and work it on out.
(Come on ba - by) (Work it on out)
A7 D G
1. Well, work it on out, (Work it on out)
2,3. You know you twist, lit - tle girl, (Twist lit - tle girl)
A7 D G A7
You know you look so good. (Look so good) You know you got me
You know you twist so fine. (Twist so fine) Come on and twist a lit - tle
D G A7
go - in' now, (Got me goin') Just like I knew you would.
clos - er now, And let me know that you're
(Twist a lit - tle clos - er)

D
G
To Coda
1 A7
2 A7
(Like I knew you would) Well, shake it up ba-
mine. (Let me know you're mine)
D G A G A D G
A G A D G A G A
D G A G A
Ah
Ah

A7
D.S. al Coda
Ah Ah Ah
Shake it up ba -
CODA
A7
D
G
Well, shake it, shake it, shake it, ba - by, now,
(Shake it up ba -
A7
D
G
A
Well, shake it, shake it, shake it, ba-by now.
- by.)
(Shake it up, ba - by.)
Ah
A7
D
Dmaj9
Ah Ah Ah

UNDER THE BOARDWALK

Words and Music by ARTIE RESNICK
and KENNY YOUNG

Copyright © 1964 by Alley Music Corp. and Trio Music Co., Inc.
Copyright Renewed
International Copyright Secured All Rights Reserved
Used by Permission

G C

- proof. Un - der the board - walk,
they sell. Un - der the board - walk,

mf

G

down by the sea, yeah, On a
down by the sea, yeah, On a

D7 G

blan - ket with my ba - by's where I'll be.
blan - ket with my ba - by's where I'll be.

Em

(Un - der the board - walk) Out of the sun (Un - der the

D
board - walk) We'll be hav - in' some fun (Un - der the
Em
board - walk) Peo - ple walk - in' a - bove
(Un - der the
D
board - walk) we'll be fall - in' in love Un - der the
(un - der the
Em
1,2
3
board - walk, board - walk. From the walk.
board - walk, board - walk. Instrumental walk.
mp

WALK THIS WAY

Words and Music by STEVEN TYLER
and JOE PERRY

Copyright © 1975 Daksel LLC
All Rights Administered by Sony/ATV Music Publishing, 8 Music Square West, Nashville, TN 37203
International Copyright Secured All Rights Reserved

ain't seen noth in' till you're down on a muf-fin, then you're
"Hey, did - dle, did - dle, with your kit - ty in the mid - dle of the
three young la - dies in the school gym lock - er when I
"Hey, did - dle, did - dle, with your kit - ty in the mid - dle of the
sure to be a chang-in' your ways." I meet a
swing like you did - n't care. So I
no - ticed they was look - in' at me. I was a
swing like you did - n't care. So I
cheer - lead - er, was a real young bleed - er, oh, the
took a big chance at the high school dance with a
high school los - er, nev - er made it with a la - dy till the
took a big chance at the high school dance with a
times I could remi - i - nisce; 'cause the
miss - y who was read - y to play. Was it
boys told me some-thin' I missed. Then my
miss - y who was read - y to play. Was it

best things of lov - in' with her sis - ter and her cous - in on - ly
me she was fool - in', 'cause she knew what she was do - in' when I
next door neigh-bor with a daugh-ter had a fa - vor, so I
1,3
A
start - ed with a lit - tle kiss like this.
knowed love was here to stay
gave her just a lit - tle kiss like this.
no chord

A
2,4
C
when she told me to
She told me to
walk this way,
F7
1,2,3
walk this way,
4
C
and just gim-me a kiss

A
To Coda
like this!
no chord
A
D.S. al Coda
CODA
no chord
Repeat and Fade

WHITE ROOM

Words and Music by JACK BRUCE
and PETE BROWN

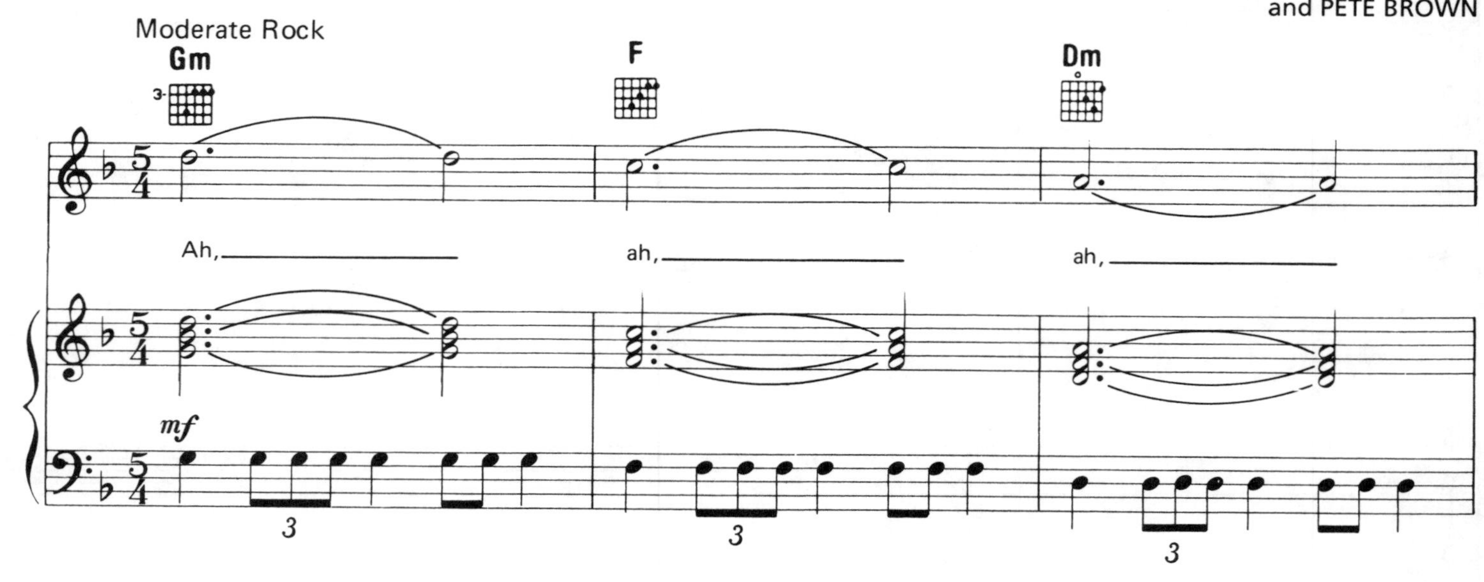

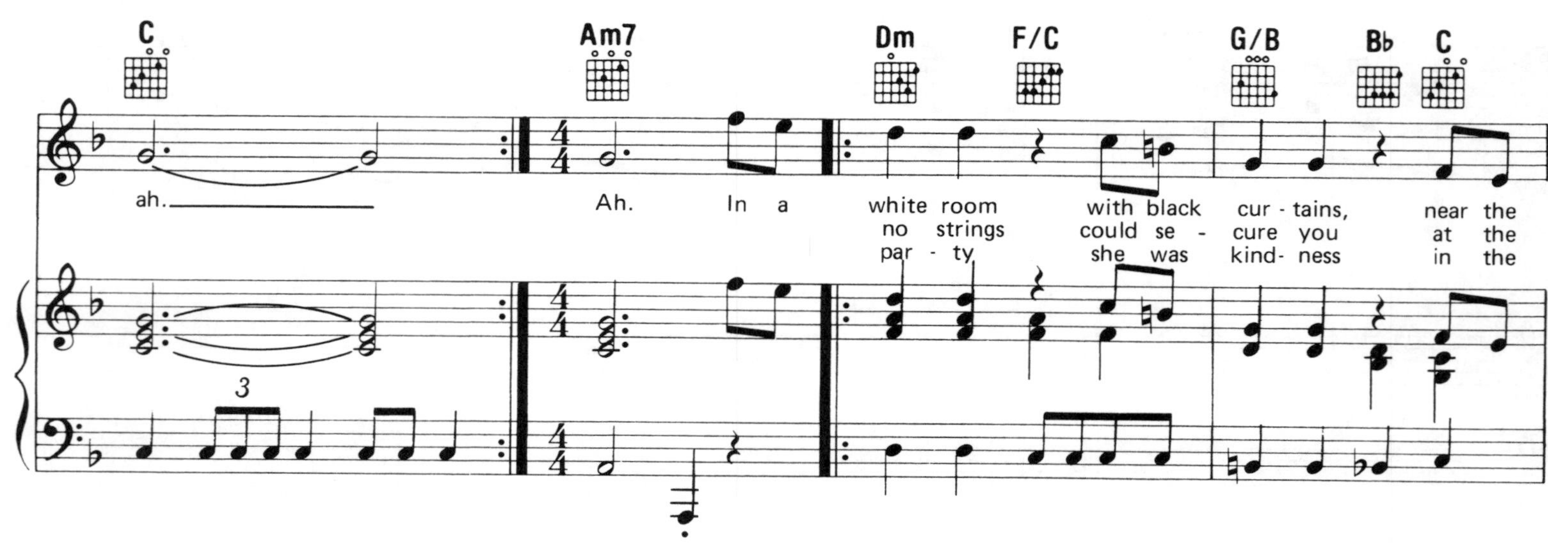

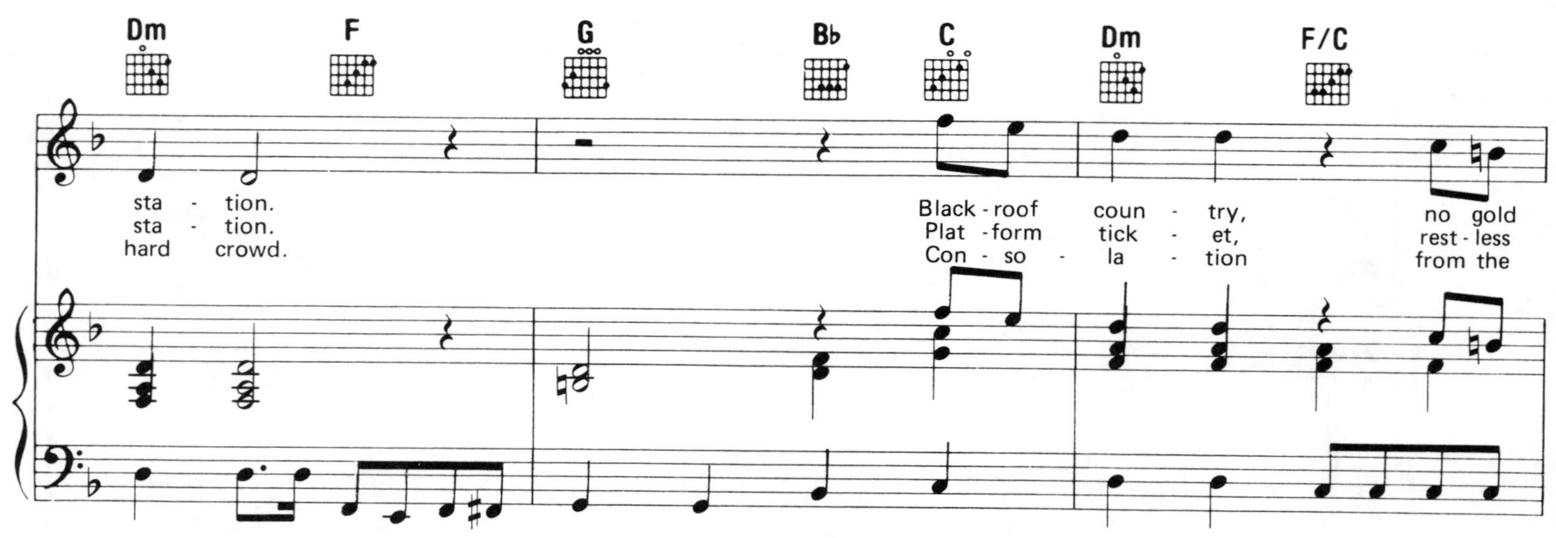

Copyright © 1968 by Dratleaf Ltd.
Copyright Renewed
All Rights Administered by Unichappell Music Inc.
International Copyright Secured All Rights Reserved

G/B Bb C Dm F G Bb C
pave - ments, tir - ed star - lings. Sil - ver
die - sels, good-bye win - dows. I walked
old wound now for - got - ten. Yel - low
Dm F/C G/B Bb C Dm F
hor - ses, run-down moon - beams in your dark eyes.
in - to such a sad time at the sta - tion.
ti - gers crouched in jun - gles in her dark eyes.
G Bb C Dm F/C G/B Bb C
Dawn-light smiles on your leav - ing, my con -
As I walked out, felt my own need just be -
She's just dress - ing good-bye win - dows, tir - ed
Dm F G Gm C G
tent - ment. I'll wait in this place where the
gin - ning. I'll wait in the queue when the
star - lings. I'll sleep in this place with the

Bb
A
C
G
sun nev - er shines,
trains come back.
lone - ly crowd,
Wait in this place
Lie with you
Lie in the dark
where the
Bb
C
1,2 D
Guitar Tacet
shad - ows run from them - selves.
You said
At the
3 D
Gm
F
selves.
Ah, ah,
Dm
C
Am7
Dm
ah, ah.
Ah.

A WHITER SHADE OF PALE

Words and Music by KEITH REID
and GARY BROOKER

© Copyright 1967 (Renewed) Onward Music Ltd., London, England
TRO - Essex Music, Inc., New York, controls all publication rights for the U.S.A. and Canada
International Copyright Secured
All Rights Reserved Including Public Performance For Profit
Used by Permission

C
C/B
Am
Em
F
Dm/E
the crowd called out for more. The room was hum - ming hard -
and forced her to a - gree. Say - ing, "You must be the mer -
and would not let her be one of six - teen ves - tal vir -
Dm7
G
G/F
Em
G7
- er as the ceil - ing flew a - way.
- maid who took Nep - tune for a ride,"
- gins who were leav - ing for the coast.
C
C/B
Am
Em
When we called out for an - oth - er drink
but she smiled at me so sad - ly
And al - though my eyes were o - pen
F
Dm/E
Dm7
Em/G
the wait - er brought a tray.
that my an - ger straight - way died.
they might just as well been closed.
And so it

C6 C/B Am C F F/E

was ___ that la - ter ___ as the mill - er told his

Dm7 C G/F Em G7

tale, ___ That her face at first just ghost - ly turned a

C F To Coda 1 C G7

whit - er ___ shade of pale. ___

2 C G7 D.C. al Coda

pale. ___

CODA C

pale. ___

WILD THING

Words and Music by
CHIP TAYLOR

© 1965 (Renewed 1993) EMI BLACKWOOD MUSIC INC.
All Rights Reserved International Copyright Secured Used by Permission

F
Eb
F
Eb
F
WILD THING, I ___ think I love you. But I wan - na know
WILD THING, I ___ think you move me. But I wan - na know
Eb
F
Eb
F
___ for sure. Come on and hold me tight. _
___ for sure. Come on and hold me tight. _
Eb
F
Eb
F
C
F
Bb
I love you.
You move me.
C
Bb
F
Bb
C

F
B♭
C
B♭
F
B♭
WILD THING,
You make my heart sing.
C
B♭
F
B♭
C
B♭
You make eve - ry - thing groov - y.
F
B♭
C
Repeat and Fade
WILD THING.

WOOLY BULLY

Words and Music by
DOMINGO SAMUDIO

© 1964, 1965 Beckie Publishing Co., Inc.
Copyright Renewed
All Rights Reserved

And a wool - y jaw
Wool - y
A♭7
Bul - ly
Wool - y
E♭7
Bul - ly
Wool - y
B♭7
Bul - ly
Wool - y
A♭7
Bul - ly
Wool - y

Additional Lyrics

2. Hatty told Matty
Let's don't take no chance,
Let's not be L 7
Come and learn to dance
Wooly bully — wooly bully —
Wooly bully — wooly bully — wooly bully.

3 Matty told Hatty
That's the thing to do,
Get yo' someone really
To pull the wool with you —
Wooly bully — wooly bully
Wooly bully — wooly bully — wooly bully.

YOU KEEP ME HANGIN' ON

Words and Music by EDWARD HOLLAND,
LAMONT DOZIER and BRIAN HOLLAND

© 1966 (Renewed 1994) JOBETE MUSIC CO., INC.
All Rights Controlled and Administered by EMI BLACKWOOD MUSIC INC. on behalf of STONE AGATE MUSIC (A Division of JOBETE MUSIC CO., INC.)
All Rights Reserved International Copyright Secured Used by Permission

Em/G
Em/D
Fmaj7
Esus
me but you keep me hang - in' on.
me you just keep me hang - in' on.
1
B♭/C
F
Why do you keep a com - in' a - round
play - ing with my heart?
C
B♭/C
Why don't - cha get out of my life
F
C
Em/B
G
and let me make a new start?
Let me get o - ver you the

E
2
B♭/C
way you've got - ten o - ver me.
You say al - though
we broke up you still wan - na be just friends.
F
C
B♭/C
F
But how can we still be friends when see - ing you on - ly breaks my
A
E
heart a - gain?
(Spoken:) And there ain't nothing I can do about it.

A
Em/G
Em/D
Set me free why don't cha ba - by, get out my life why don't
Fmaj7
Esus
B♭/C
cha ba - by. You claim you still care for me but your
F
C
B♭/C
heart and soul needs to be free. Now that you've got
F
C
Em/B
your free - dom you wan - na still hold on to me.

G
E
You don't want me for your - self so let me find some-bod - y else.
Am
A
Em/G
Why don't cha be a man a - bout it
Em/D
Fmaj7
Esus
A
and set me free. Now you don't care a
Em/G
Em/D
Fmaj7
Esus
thing a - bout me, you're just us - ing me. Boy,

A
Em/G
Em/D
get out, get out - ta my life and let me sleep at night,
Fmaj7
Esus
A
Em/G
'cause you don't real - ly love me, you just keep
Em/D
Fmaj7
Esus
A
me hang - ing on.
'Cause you don't real - ly need
Am/E
Em/G
F
Am
me, so let me be, set me free.

YOU GIVE LOVE A BAD NAME

Words and Music by JON BON JOVI,
RICHIE SAMBORA and DESMOND CHILD

Copyright © 1986 PolyGram International Publishing, Inc., Bon Jovi Publishing, New Jersey Underground Music Inc., EMI April Music Inc. and Desmobile Music Co., Inc.
All Rights for Desmobile Music Co., Inc. Controlled and Administered by EMI April Music Inc.
International Copyright Secured All Rights Reserved

An

Cm
3fr.
an - gel's smile is what you sell. You prom - ise me heav - en, then
paint your smile on your lips. Blood – red nails on your

put me through hell. Chains of love got a hold on me. When
fin - ger – tips. A school boy's dream, you act so shy. Your

F
pas - sion's a pris - on, you can't break free.
ver - y first kiss was your first kiss good - bye.
Oh, you're a
Cm
3fr.
load - ed gun.
B♭
F
Oh, there's no - where to run, no one can save me, the
G
Cm
3fr.
A♭
4fr.
B♭
Cm
3fr.
dam - age is done. Shot through the heart and you're to blame.

Ab
4fr.
Bb
Eb5
Cm
3fr.
You give love a bad name, bad name. I play my part and you
play your game.
You give love a bad name, bad name. Oh,
you give love, a bad name.
1.
2.
Bb/C
You

Cm 3fr.
Ab 4fr.
Bb
Cm 3fr.
Ab 4fr.
Bb
Shot through the heart and you're to blame. You give love a
Eb5
C
Ab 4fr.
Bb
Cm 3fr.
bad name, bad name. I play my part and you play your game.
Repeat and fade
Ab 4fr.
Bb
Eb5
Cm 3fr.
Ab 4fr.
Bb
You give love a bad name, bad name. You give love,
Eb5
Cm 3fr.
Ab 4fr.
Bb
Eb5
Cm 3fr.
you give love a bad name.